# ᴊRISH
## VITAL RECORDS
*from*
## The Scots Magazine
### 1739 - 1826

## David Dobson

CLEARFIELD

Printed for Clearfield Company by
Genealogical Publishing Company
Baltimore, Maryland
2013


ISBN 978-0-8063-5636-5

*Made in the United States of America*

# INTRODUCTION

'The Scots Magazine' is probably the world's oldest magazine still in print. It was originally published as a monthly journal in Edinburgh in 1739 and continued in print until 1826 when printing was suspended. Later in the nineteenth century the magazine was re-issued and it is still in print although in a much different format.

The first issue was released in February 1739 and its frontispiece stated that it contained "a General View of the Religion, Politicks, Entertainment, etc, in Great Britain; and a succinct account of Publick Affairs, Foreign and Domestick". Among its regular features were announcements of births, marriages and deaths throughout the British Isles and abroad. Among such announcements were a substantial number pertaining to Ireland, these have been extracted and formed into this genealogical source book which provides a unique source for family historians. The referencing supplies the volume numbers and the page numbers where the entries are located.

David Dobson

Dundee, Scotland

**ABBOTT, Mrs ELIZABETH,** aged 102, died in Maragall, Lisburn, on 10 October 1815. [SM.77.879]

**ABERCROMBY, Captain WILLIAM,** of the Invalids, died in the Invalid Barracks, Dublin, in 1802. [SM.64.276]

**ACHESON, ARTHUR,** Earl of Gosford, Viscount Gosford of Markethill, Governor of Armagh, died in Bath on 13 January 1807. [SM.69.80]

**ADAIR, Reverend WILLIAM,** LL.D. rector of Fermony, died there on 19 August 1814. [SM.76.878]

**ADAMS, ......,** Major of Otway's Regiment of Foot, died in Dublin on 8 July 1749. [SM.11.350]

**ADAMS, Mrs,** aged 120, died in Drogheda in November 1768. [SM.30.671]

**ADLERCRON, Lieutenant General JOHN,** Colonel of the 39th Regiment, died near Blackrock in Ireland, on 25 July 1766. [SM.28.390]

**AGAR, ELLIS,** Countess of Brandon, aged 81, died in Dublin on 9 March 1789. 'She was married in 1726 to Sir Theobald Burke, afterwards Lord Viscount Mayo, and some years after his death to Francis, Lord Athenry, the premier Baron of Ireland after whose death in 1758 she was created Baroness of Brandon, the first peeress in her own right in Ireland'. [SM.51.153]

**AGAR, Mrs MARY,** aged 106, died at Ringwood in Ireland on 24 March 1771. [SM.33.331]

**AGAR, ......,** Lord Viscount Clifden, died in Ireland 1788, he was created a Peer in 1780, joint postmaster of Ireland, he was succeeded in title and estate by his eldest son Henry William Agar, the Member of Parliament for County Kilkenny. [SM.51.52]

**Aghrim, Lord,** eldest son of the Earl of Athlone, married Miss Munter, in Utrecht in 1789. [SM.51.205]

**AGNEW, Captain GEORGE,** brother of the late Sir Andrew Agnew, died in Dublin on 14 March 1773. [SM.35.165]

**AGNEW, Captain JOHN,** brother to the deceased Sir Andrew Agnew baronet, died in Longford on 26 December 1780. [SM.42.673]

**AGNEW, WILLIAM,** Lieutenant Colonel late of the 24th Regiment, died at Healthfield on 10 June 1784. [SM.46.334]

**AGNEW, Mrs,** wife of Captain John Agnew, brother of the late Sir Andrew Agnew, died in Longford on 4 March 1773. [SM.35.165]

**ALAND, Sir JOHN FORTESCUE,** a judge of Common Pleas, Baron Fortescue of Credan, died on 18 December 1746. [SM.8.598]

**Aldborough, the Earl of,** died in Dublin on 19 June 1777. [SM.39.390]

**Aldborough, the Countess Dowager of,** aged 90, died in Dublin on 11 March 1796. [SM.58.289]

**ALEXANDER, Reverend JOHN,** aged 41, pastor of the Reformed Presbyterian congregation in Belfast, and teacher of mathematics in the Belfast Academy, died in Belfast on 10 November 1823. [SM.92.768]

**ALLEN, JOHN,** Lord Viscount Allen, died in Stillorgan, Ireland, on 25 May 1745. [SM.7.249]

**ALLEN, Lord JOHN,** an Irish peer, died at his seat near Naas on 26 January 1752. [SM.14.101]

**ALLEN, JOHN,** 'one of the oldest merchants in Dublin, and a Director of the Bank of Ireland since its first inception' died in Dublin on 10 January 1807. [SM.69.79]

**ALLEN, JOSHUA,** Viscount Allen, Baron of Stillorgan, died at Stillorgan in Ireland, 4 December 1742. [SM.4.582]

**ALLEN, ......,** son of Samuel Allen of Ballymeny, was born in Edinburgh on 25 February 1808. [SM.70.316]

**ALLEN, Lady Viscountess-Dowager,** of Ireland, died in London on 4 March 1758. [SM.20.110]

**ALLEY, Reverend PETER,** aged 110, died in Ballyhaggiton, Queen's County, on 22 August 1763. 'He was rector of the parish of Donamow 73 years ..... he was great grandson to William Alley bishop of Exeter in the reign of Queen Elizabeth. He was twice married and had by his first wife 16 children, and by his last wife 17'. [SM.25.472]

**Altamont, JOHN, Earl of,** died at his seat in Westport in June 1776. [SM.38.395]

**Altamont, PETER, Earl of,** Viscount Westport, Baron Mount Eagle, aged 50, died in Westport, County Mayo, on 28 December 1780. He was succeeded by his eldest son John Browne, commonly called Lord Westport. [SM.42.54]

**ANDERSON, ISABELLA,** daughter of John Anderson of Fermoy, Ireland, died in New Abbey on 4 July 1819. [SM.84.200]

**ANDERSON, JAMES DOWLING,** died at Cullinagh House, Queen's County, in December 1804. [SM.67.77]

**ANDERSON, Sir JAMES C.**, of Fermoy, County Cork, married Caroline Shaw, third daughter of the late Robert Shaw in Dublin, and sister to Robert Shaw Member of Parliament for Dublin, in Seafortie, County Down, on 20 April 1815. [SM.77.399]

**ANDERSON, JOHN,** from Cork, married Miss Sempill, daughter of James Sempill, MD, in Waterford in August 1791. [SM.53.466]

**ANDERSON, SAMUEL JONES BERNARD,** died at Cullinagh House, Queen's County, in December 1804. [SM.67.77]

**ANDERSON, ......,** daughter of Sir J. Anderson, was born in Fermoy House, Ireland, on 11 October 1817. [SM.80.1397]

**ANDERSON, ......,** daughter of Captain Robert Anderson of the 91st Regiment, was born in Enniskillen on 2 February 1821. [SM.87.292]

**Annesley, ANNE, Countess of,** died in Belfast on 30 June 1822. [SM.90.270]

**ANNESLEY, Major General ARTHUR,** third son of the Earl of Annesley, married Elizabeth Mahon, only daughter of John Mahon of Besborough, Tipperary, at Ballymacey Church, Tipperary, on 28 December 1814. [SM.77.159]

**ANNESLEY, FRANCES CAROLINE,** second daughter of the Earl of Mountnorris, and sister of Viscount Valencia, married James Wedderburn Webster of Clapham, Surrey, on 8 December 1810. [SM.73.76]

**ANNESLEY, Lord Baron HENRY,** of Tenelick, formerly Member of Parliament for County Longford, died in Dublin on 5 June 1793. [SM.55.308]

**ANNESLEY, Mrs MARGARET,** aged 122, died in Newcastle, County Dublin, on 20 November 1752. [SM.14.558]

**ANNESLEY, Sir RICHARD,** Viscount Valentia in Ireland, aged 71, died at his seat in County Wexford on 14 February 1761. [SM.23.112]

**Annesley, RICHARD, Earl of,** Viscount Gerawly and Baron Castlewilliam, died in Dublin on 8 November 1824. [SM.94.768]

**ANNESLEY, WILLIAM,** Viscount Gerawly and Baron Annesley of Castle William in County Down, died at Clontarff near Dublin on 12 September 1770. [SM.32.558]

**ANNESLEY, Mr,** eldest son of Lord Annesley, married Miss Grove, in Ireland on 8 February 1766. [SM.28.166]

**Annesley, the Earl of,** died in Ireland in 1797 'in a skirmish with the defenders'. [SM.59.215]

**ANNESLEY, ......,** daughter of Dr Annesley of the Scots Greys, was born in Dundalk on 3 November 1818. [SM.82.486]

**Annesley, the Earl of,** Viscount Glerawley, and Baron of Castle Wellen, died at the Giant's Causeway in 1825. [SM.96.640]

**ANSTRUTHER, ......,** son of Lieutenant Colonel Anstruther, was born in Dublin on 11 January 1803. 'The child lived only a few hours'. [SM.65.72]

**ANSTRUTHER, ......,** daughter of Colonel Robert Anstruther, Adjutant General of Ireland, was born in Dublin in March 1808. [SM.70.316]

**Antrim, the EARL of,** married Miss Plunket, granddaughter of Colonel Stafford, in Belan, County Kildare, in 1739. [SM.2.46]

**Antrim, .....,** son and heir of the Earl of Antrim was born 4 November 1749. [SM.11.559]

**Antrim, .....,** son of the Earl of Antrim, was born in Dublin on 30 June 1751 but died soon after. [SM.13.357]

**Antrim, the Countess of,** died at Glenarm on 14 January 1755. [SM.17.52]

**ARABINE, JOHN,** Colonel of Colonel Campbell's Dragoons, died in Dublin on 12 February 1758, onlyson of the late Colonel Arabine. [SM.20.110]

**ARBUCKLE, Reverend JAMES,** aged 37, rector of Barragh, County Wexford, died in Donaghadee on 29 January 1810. [SM.73.159]

**ARBUTHNOTT, ROBERT,** a Lieutenant in the 23rd Light Dragoons, married Miss Vesey, only daughter of the late William Vesey of Farnichill, in Belfast in 1802. [SM.64.181]

**ARCHDALL, Reverend MERVYN,** aged 68, MA, a member of the Royal Irish Academy, author of Monasticum Hibernicum, and Lodge's Peerage, died in Slane, County Meath, on 6 August 1791. [SM.53.415]

**ARCHER, JOHN,** formerly a book-seller in Dublin, died on 13 July 1811. [SM.73.639]

**ARCHER, ......,** a blacksmith, aged 80, married Mrs Ruth Redding aged 70, in Cork on 4 February 1762. 'The courtship began, the match was concluded, and the marriage consummated in a few hours'. [SM.24.111]

**Arran, the Earl of,** married Miss Underwood, in Ireland in February 1780. [SM.42.109]

**Arran, the Earl of,** a Knight of St Patrick, died in Dublin on 8 October 1809. [SM.71.879]

**Ashbrook, Lord Viscount HENRY,** died in Dublin in June 1752. [SM.14.366]

**Ashbrook, Viscountess Dowager ELIZABETH,** of Ireland, daughter of the late General Tatton, died in London on 9 February 1759. [SM.21.101]

**ASTLE, Major,** aged 100, died in Carlow on 1 April 1773. [SM.35.278]

**Athenry, ......,** son and heir apparent of Lord Athenry, was born in Dublin on 21 September 1753. [SM.15.525]

**Athenry, ......,** son of Lord Athenry an Irish peer, was born in Dublin on 5 February 1755. [SM.17.108]

**Athlone, ......,** daughter of the Countess of Athlone, was born in the Hague on 2 December 1819. [SM.85.93]

**Athlone, ......** son of the Countess of Athlone, was born in the Hague on 21 November 1821. [SM.87.93]

**Athlone, the Earl of,** died in the Hague on 31 October 1823. [SM.92.768]

**AUDLEY, .....,** son of Lady Audley, was born in Cork on 8 November 1819. [SM.85.92]

**AYLMER, RICHARD,** aged 103, died at Chapelizod, Dublin, on 19 August 1761. [SM.23.558]

**AYLMER, Lady,** aged 60, of Ireland, died in Greenwich, 1750. [SM.12.54]

**AYLMER, Miss,** daughter of Sir Fitzgerald Aylmer, baronet, married Sir John Hort of Hertland, baronet, Consul General at the Portuguese Court, at Donadea Castle, County Kildare, in 1789. [SM.51.517]

**BABINGTON, RALPH,** of Greenfoot, died in Londonderry on 10 February 1806. [SM.67.238]

**BAGSHAWE, SAMUEL,** Colonel of the 98th Regiment of Foot, died in Ireland on 20 October 1762. [SM.24.568]

**BAILLIE, JOHN,** of Dunean, Colonel of the Loyal Inverness Regiment of Fencibles, died in Kilkenny on 26 January 1797. [SM.59.244]

**BAINHAM, JANE,** aged 106, died in Ringsend on 25 January 1766. [SM.28.55]

**BALFOUR, ......,** daughter of Colonel Balfour of the 3rd Regiment, was born at Sea View near Belfast, on 31 July 1819. [SM.84.292]

**BALL, JOHN,** aged 75, a Captain of Churchill's Royal Regiment of Dragoons, died in Dublin on 8 March 1755. [SM.17.160]

**Bandon, the Countess of,** only daughter of Richard, Earl of Shannon, was born in Castle Bernard near Cork on 8 July 1815. [SM.77.719]

**BANNERS, JOHN,** of the 23<sup>rd</sup> Light Dragoons, married Mary Ann Fraser, daughter of Robert Murray Fraser of Mountjoy Square, in Dublin on 2 August 1814. [SM.76.716]

**BARCLAY, JOHN,** son of Robert Barclay, a merchant and a Quaker, died in Dublin on 8 June 1751. [SM.13.309]

**BAREY, .....,** twins, children of Michael Barey of Mullogh, County Clare, were born on 3 February 1777, their mother was aged 62. [SM.39.110]

**BARNARD, Dr WILLIAM,** Bishop of Derry, died in London on 11 January 1768. [SM.30.54]

**BARNEWALL, GEORGE,** only brother of Lord Kingsland, died in Dublin in May 1771. [SM.33.390]

**BARNWELL, NICHOLAS,** Baron Trimleston, aged 85, died in Turvey House on 16 April 1813. [SM.75.400]

**BARNWELL, ......,** Lord Trimlestown, died in Dublin on 7 April 1746. [SM.8.198]

**BARRET, J.,** aged 76, married Mrs Masters, aged 82, in Christ Church, Cork, in 1810. [SM.72.877]

**BARRET, Dr JOHN,** Vice Provost of Trinity College, Dublin, died in Dublin on 15 November 1821. [SM.88.620]

**BARRINGTON, EDWARD,** of the 5<sup>th</sup> Dragoon Guards, son of Sir Jonah Barrington a judge of the Court of Admiralty of Ireland, married Anna Hamilton Blake, third daughter of Netterville Blake of Berming House, County Galway, and grand-niece of Viscount Netterville, in Tuam Cathedral on 19 July 1824. [SM.94.255]

**BARROW, ROBERT,** aged 105, died in Bridewell Lane, Cork, in July 1767. [SM.29.446]

**BARRY, ARTHUR,** third son of the Earl of Barrymore, died in Dublin on 23 October 1770. [SM.32.575]

**BARRY, Sir EDWARD,** MD, Physician to the Forces in Ireland, for many years a member of the Irish House of Commons, died in Bath on 25 March 1776. [SM.38.221]

**BARRY, JAMES,** Earl of Barrymore, died at Castle Lyons in County Cork on 4 January 1748. He served in Spain during Queen Anne's wars. He was succeeded by his eldest son James, Lord Viscount Bateman. [SM.10.50]

**BARRY, RICHARD,** 7$^{TH}$ Earl of Barrymore, Member of Parliament for Heytesbury, Wiltshire, and an officer in the Queen's Regiment, died near Folkestone when escorting French prisoners to Dover on 6 March 1793. [SM.55.153]

**Barrymore, the Dowager Countess of,** died in Dublin on 2 December 1788. [SM.50.622]

**Bantry, ......,** son of Lord Bantry was born in Cork on 30 April 1810. [SM.72.477]

**BASSET, Major RICHARD,** of Sir John Bruce-Hope's Regiment of Foot, died in Youghal in March 1746. [SM.8.150]

**BATEMAN, JOHN,** of Killern, County Kerry, married the Countess of Ross, 1770. [SM.32.574]

**BATES, WILLIAM,** aged 98, died near Clonmel in December 1777. [SM.39.679]

**BATTIER, GEORGE,** late of HMS Resolution, died at Mount Merrion, near Dublin, in 1804. 'He circumnavigated the globe with Captain Cook, and was present with him at his death'. [SM.67.158]

**BEAMISH, WILLIAM,** eldest son of William Beamish of Beaumont, Ireland, married Mary de Courcy, daughter of Lord Kinsale, at Lochnaw Castle on 15 September 1814. [SM.76.799]

**BEATY, JAMES,** aged 112, born in Noyalty, County Meath, a farmer though earlier a weaver, died at Drumcondra near Dublin in 1814. 'At the time of his death he had three sons by three different wives, the eldest 84, and the youngest 7. He was a hard drinker until he was 60, since then he uniformly drank 3 pints of porter, two glasses of whisky, walked eight miles, and shaved himself every day'. [SM.76.720]

**BEATY, WILLIAM,** aged 130, died in Dungiven on 16 February 1774. [SM.36.111]

**BECHER, .......,** daughter of William Wrixon Becher, was born in Ballygiblin, County Cork, on 4 July 1823. [SM.92.254]

**Bective, .......,** daughter of the Earl of Bective, was born in Rutland Square, Dublin, on 6 February 1824. [SM.93.382]

**Bedford, .......,** son of the Duke of Bedford, was born in Dublin Castle on 10 February 1807. [SM.69.157]

**BEERE, WILLIAM,** of Ballyboy, County Tipperary, aged 85, married Mrs Guard of Mallow, aged 91, in Ireland in February 1756. [SM.18.108]

**Begg, .......,** daughter of the Earl of Begg, was born in Dublin in 1802. [SM.64.615]

**BELL, GEORGE,** aged 74, Captain of the late General Ponsonby's Regiment, died in Ireland on 26 December 1758. 'He served in all the campaigns of Queen Anne, George I, and George II, and was at the Battle of Preston also served during the late rebellion'. [SM.21.51]

**BELL, Sir THOMAS,** MD, died in Dublin on 2 December 1789. [SM.51.621]

**Bellamont, the Earl of,** married Lady Emily Fitzgerald, sister of the Duke of Leinster, in Carton House, Ireland, in August 1774. [SM.36.447]

**BELLMOUR, JAMES,** aged 31, born in Glasgow, manager of a company of comedians in the west of Scotland and north of Ireland, died at Killileegh, Ireland, on 17 January 1812. [S,.74.238]

**Belmore, ........,** daughter of the Earl of Belmore, was born in Dublin on 23 August 1806. [SM.67.726]

**Belvedere, the Earl of,** Quartermaster of HM Forces in Ireland, died at Belvedere, County West Meath, on 21 November 1774. [SM.36.623]

**Belvedere, the Earl of,** married Miss Bloomfield, second daughter of the late John Bloomfield of Redwood in August 1775. [SM.37.462]

**Belvedere, the Earl of,** died in Dublin on 12 May 1814. [SM.76.560]

**BENNET, ALEXANDER,** aged 125, a former trooper in the Duke of Monmouth's army at the battle of Bothwell Bridge in 1679, he was at the Siege of Derry, also at the battle of the Boyne and the battle of Angrim, died at Rathfryland, County Down, on 19 August 1749. [SM.11.406]

**BENNET, JOHN,** second Justice of the Court of King's Bench in Ireland, died in Dublin on 25 December 1791. [SM.53.49]

**BERESFORD, JOHN,** Member of Parliament for Waterford, died in Ireland on 15 October 1805. [SM.67.886]

**BERESFORD, Sir MARCUS,** Earl of Tyrone, aged 70, died in Dublin on 4 April 1763. 'He is succeeded in titles and estate by his son George'. [SM.25.301]

**BERESFORD, MARCUS,** Member of Parliament, son of John Beresford, married Lady Frances Leeson, daughter of the late, and sister of the present Earl of Milltown, in Dublin on 24 February 1791. [SM.53.151]

**BERESFORD, MARCUS,** Member of Parliament for Dungarven, at at the seat of J. Beresford in Abbeville, Ireland, in 1797. [SM.59.931]

**BERESFORD, Mrs,** aged 103, grand-aunt to the Marquis of Waterford, died in Dublin in 1794. [SM.58.71]

**BERFORD, ANNE MARIA,** daughter of John Fitzwilliam Berford in Dublin, married David Brown of Rawflat, in Jedburgh, Scotland, on 8 June 1825. [SM.96.127]

**BERNARD, JAMES,** Member of Parliament for County Cork, died on 10 July 1790. [SM.52.363]

**BERNARD, ......,** Captain of Waldegrave's Regiment of Foot, died in Dublin on 8 July 1751. [SM.13.357]

**BETHUNE, Brigade Major LINDSAY,** son of Henry Bethune of Kilconquhar, Fife, married Miss Forster, only daughter of Forster Hill Forster of Forrest, County Dublin, there on 28 February 1807. [SM.69.236]

**BETTESWORTH, Colonel,** of the Royal Irish Artillery, died in Dublin on 2 February 1790. [SM.52.102]

**BIAN, DAVID,** aged 117, died in Tinnerane on 14 March 1776. [SM.38.163]

**BINDON, FRANCIS,** 'one of the best painters and architects Ireland ever produced' died in his chariot on his way from Dublin to the country on 2 June 1765. [SM.27.335]

**BINDON, Dr NICHOLAS,** of Limerick, married Cecilia Ferguson, daughter of Walter Ferguson, a writer in Edinburgh, on 12 June 1790. [SM.52.309]

**BINGHAM, JOHN,** of Newbroke, County Mayo, married Miss Yelverton, only daughter of Lord Chief Baron Yelverton, in Ireland on 20 May 1791. [SM.53.257]

**BIRMINGHAM, FRANCIS,** Lord Athunry, First Baron of Ireland, died in Dublin on 3 March 1750. [SM.12.158]

**BIRMINGHAM, THOMAS,** son and heir to Lord Athunry, married Miss Dailly, daughter of Peter Dailly, in Dublin on 30 December 1749. [SM.12.55]

**BLACK, JOHN,** surgeon of HMS La Prompt, died at the Cove of Cork in 1800. [SM.62.652]

**BLACKFORD, Mrs,** grand-daughter of the Earl of Darnley, died in Dublin in 1817. [SM.80.502]

**BLACKHALL, Sir THOMAS,** senior Alderman of Dublin, died there on 6 May 1796. [SM.58.361]

**BLACKNEY, PATRICK,** aged 104, died in Carrickfergus on 1 August 1781. 'he was formerly a captain in the army and served under the Duke of Marlborough'. [SM.43.446]

**BLAIN, WILLIAM,** aged 90, died in Donaghadee on 21 December 1816, his wife Mary, aged 93, predeceased him by two weeks. [SM.79.159]

**BLAIR, PIERCE FREDERICK,** brother of the late Sir D. Blair, died of typhus at Belle Cottage, Ireland, on 22 November 1817. He was uncle to Frederick Gustavus Moore of Dublin. [SM.81.95]

**BLAIR, ROBERT,** a Captain of the 68th Regiment, died in Armagh on 27 March 1799. [SM.61.211]

**BLAIR, .......,** son of Captain Blair of the 4th Dragoon Guards, was born in Dublin on 2 April 1798. [SM.60.363]

**BLAKE, JOSEPH,** father of Lord Walscourt and the Countess Dowager of Errol, died in his seat of Ardfrey, Ireland, in 1806. [SM.67.239]

**BLAKE, Reverend Dr.,** titular Primate of Ireland, died in Galway in 1787. [SM.49.622]

**BLAKENEY, DAVID,** 'the matros who lately made so much noise in Dublin', died in the north of Ireland on 11 September 1768. [SM.30.502]

**BLAKENEY, General GRICE,** Colonel of the 4th Royal Veteran Battalion, died in 1816 near Four-Mile-Water, County Waterford. [SM.78.960]

**BLAKENEY, Lieutenant General WILLIAM,** aged 91, Colonel of the Inneskilling Regiment of Foot, died 20 September 1761. 'For his brave defence of Fort St Philip's in 1756 he was created a Knight of the Bath and a peer of Ireland. [SM.23.558]

**BLAKENEY, ROBERT,** aged 114, a former army officer, died near Armagh on 22 June 1782. [SM.44.390]

**BLANEY, Lord CHARLES,** Dean of Kildare, died in Dublin on 29 September 1761. [SM.23.559]

**BLANEY, Lady,** aged 85, died in Dublin on 28 September 1790. 'She was the mother of the Countess of Clermont'. [SM.52.464]

**BLAQUIERE, Sir JOHN,** married Miss Eleanor Dobson, heiress of Robert Dobson of Ann Grove, Yorkshire, in Dublin on 30 December 1775. [SM.38.53]

**BLAYNEY, Lady,** died in Ireland on 9 April 1756. [SM.18.198]

**BLENNERHASSET, ARTHUR,** a Justice of the King's bench in Ireland, died in Dublin on 3 January 1758. [SM.20.51]

**BLENNERHASSET, ARTHUR,** only son of Gerald Blennerhasset of Riddlestown, County Limerick, drowned in Lake Killarney on 2 October 1775. [SM.37.582]

**BLENNERHASSET, Colonel JOHN,** of Balliferdy, died at Oak Park, County Kerry, in May 1775. 'he was knight of the shire from the reign of Queen Anne to his death'. [SM.37.286]

**Blensington, MARTHA, Viscountess Dowager,** aged 84, died in Ireland on 18 June 1767. [SM.29.335]

**BLEWET, PATRICK,** aged 120, died in the north of Ireland on 13 August 1770. [SM.32.458]

**BLIGH, General,** died at Brittas near Dublin on 15 September 1775. 'who, having no children, has left his fortune, upwards of £100,000 to his brother the Reverend Robert Bligh, Dean of Elphin'. [SM.37.525]

**BLOW, JAMES,** aged 83, a printer, died in Belfast on 15 August 1759. 'He was the first in the Kingdom to print the Bible'. [SM.21.445]

**BLOXHAM, DANIEL,** aged 104, died at Belturbet on 22 July 1762. [SM.24.451]

**BLUNDELL, MONTAGU,** Lord Viscount Blundell an Irish peer, died in Bath on 19 August 1756. [SM.18.416]

**BLYTH, EDWARD,** aged 97, an eminent grazier, stock-dealer, and wool-merchant, died in Louth in 1820. [SM.85.296]

**BOLTON, Dr THEOPHILUS,** Archbishop of Cashel and Primate of Munster, died in Dublin on 31 January 1744. [SM.6.98]

**BONAR, ......,** son of Thomson Bonar, was born in Rome on 24 May 1819. [SM.84.93]

**BOND, Reverend JAMES FORWARD,** Dean of Ross, married Sarah Hester Croker, daughter of the late John Croker, Surveyor General, and sister to J. W. Croker, Member of Parliament, and Secretary to the Admiralty, in Londonderry on 15 March 1815. [SM.77.318]

**BOND, Miss,** daughter of James Bond of Merrion Square, married Christopher Hely Hutchinson, son of the Secretary of State, in Dublin on 24 December 1792. [SM.55.49]

**BOULTER, Dr HUGH,** Archbishop of Armagh, Primate and Metropolitan of All Ireland, died in London in 1742. [SM.4.439]

**BOULTER, Lady,** relict of Dr Hugh Boulter late Archbishop of Ardmagh, and Pimate of All Ireland, died on 3 March 1754. [SM.16.154]

**BOURKE, Sir AYLMER,** eldest son and heir of John, Lord Viscount Mayo, an Irish Peer, died 21 July 1748. [SM.10.407]

**BOURKE, DAVID,** editor of *Saunders News Letter*, died in Dublin on 19 January 1811. [SM.73.159]

**BOURKE, JOHN,** Earl of Mayo, Lord Viscount Naas, died at the Black Rock near Dublin on 21 April 1792. 'He was married to Lady Mary Neeson, daughter of the late and sister of the present Earl of Milltown. Dying without issue he was succeeded in title and estate by the Reverend Joseph Dean Bourke, Archbishop of Tuam'. [SM.53.207]

**BOURKE, Dr JOSEPH,** Archbishop of Tuam and Earl of Mayo, died in his Palace of Tuam in 1794. [SM.56.512]

**BOURKE, MARY,** second daughter of the Archbishop of Tuam, married Lord de Clifford, in Ireland during 1789. [SM.51.204]

**Bourk-Mayo, Lord Viscount**, of Ireland, died 1741. [SM.3.571]

**BOURNE, JAMES,** of Carbolly, parish of Ganaghey, County Down, aged 106, died in 1809. [SM.71.559]

**BOURNE, ROBERT,** second son of the Reverend Richard Bourne of Holles Street, Dublin, died in Kildress, County Tyrone, on 8 June 1809. [SM.71.479]

**BOWES, Lord,** Lord Chancellor of Ireland, died in Dublin on 22 July 1767, [SM.29.390]

**BOWLES, Lieutenant General PHINEAS,** Colonel of the King's Caribiniers and Governor of Derry and Culmore Fort, died at his seat near Drogheda on 12 December 1746. [SM.8.598]

**BOYCE, Miss,** daughter and heiress of the late John Boyce, married the Earl of Darnley, in Ireland in September 1766. [SM.28.503]

**BOYD, Captain ALEXANDER,** of the 21$^{st}$ Regiment of Foot, was killed in a duel in Newry on 23 June 1807. [SM.69.639]

**BOYD, ROBERT,** aged 72, late second Justice of H.M. Court of King's Bench in Ireland, died in Dublin in 1814. [SM.76.400]

**BOYLE, CHARLES,** aged 31, Lord Viscount Dungarvon, eldest son of the Earl of Cork and Orrery, died in Bath on 16 September 1759. [SM.21.502]

**BOYLE, Lady LOUISA ISABELLA,** eldest daughter of the Earl of Cork and Orrery, married Reverend George Bridgman, on 28 July 1792. [SM.53.360]

**BOYLE, RICHARD,** aged 72, Viscount Shannon, a Field Marshal, Commander in Chief of the forces in Ireland, Colonel of the fourth troop of Horse Guards, died in London on 20 December 1740. [SM.2.578]

**BOYLE, RICHARD,** Earl of Cork, Lord High Treasurer of Ireland, born 21 April 1695, married Lady Dorothy Savile in 1721, died in London on 4 December 1753. [SM.15.581]

**BOYLE, RICHARD,** Earl of Shannon, died neat Castlemartyr, County Dublin, on 23 May 1807. [SM.69.478]

**BOYLE, Lord Viscount,** eldest son of the Earl of Shannon, married Miss Ponsonby, daughter of John Ponsonby, Speaker of the House of Commons, in Dublin on 15 December 1763. [SM.25.694]

**BOYLE, ......,** daughter of Lord Viscount Shannon, married the Earl of Middlesex on 30 October 1744. [SM.6.538]

**Boyne, Lord FREDERICK,** married Miss Smyth, daughter of Thomas Smyth, in Dublin on 15 March 1772. [SM.34.165]

**Boyne, Lord Viscount,** died in Dublin on 2 January 1772. [SM.34.50]

**Boyne, ......**son of Lord Boyne, was born in Dublin on 21 July 1774. [SM.36.447]

**BRABAZON, ANTHONY,** Earl of March, died at his seat at Kilrudery, County Wicklow, on 4 January 1790. 'He was succeeded by his eldest son William, Lord Ardee'. [SM.52.51]

**BRABAZON, CLAWORTH,** Earl of Meath, Lord Brabazon, a Privy Councillor in Ireland, died in Calais on 4 May 1763 when bound for Aix-la-Chapelle. 'He is succeeded by his brother Edward Brabazon, MP for County Dublin. [SM.25.302]

**BRADSHAW, ROBERT,** a banker and President of the Chamber of Commerce in Belfast, died there on 17 September 1819. [SM.84.391]

**BRADSTREET, Sir SAMUEL,** baronet, justice of the Court of King's Bench in Ireland, died in Booterstown, near Dublin, in 2 May 1791. [SM.53.258]

**BRADY, Mrs ANN,** aged 101, wife of a laborer, died near Rathmines, Dublin, in 1814. [SM.76.400]

**BRAGG, PHILIP,** a Lieutenant General, Colonel of the 28th Regiment of Foot, and a Major General on the Irish Establishment, died in Dublin 'in an advanced age' on 6 June 1759. [SM.21.331]

**BRANDON, Lord,** aged 73, died in Ireland on 20 January 1762. 'He is succeeded in titles and estate by his only son William Crosbie'. [SM.24.56]

**BRANAGH, EDMOND,** aged 115, died near Wicklow on 27 February 1766. [SM.28.166]

**BRAY, Reverend Dr.,** aged 74, Roman Catholic Bishop of Cashel and Emly, died in London on 9 December 1820. [SM.87.96]

**BREDIN, ALEXANDER,** former Fort Major of Edinburgh Castle, died in Letterkenny, County Donegal, on 14 August 1792. [SM.53.466]

**BRIEN, LUCINDA,** aged 108, a fruit-seller, died in Limerick in 1787. [SM.49.623]

**BRISBANE, ......,** daughter of Major General Sir Thomas Brisbane, was born in Glentown near Cork on 27 August 1820. [SM.86.381]

**BRISTOW, WILLIAM,** a Commissioner of the Excise and Revenue in Ireland, died in Dublin on 19 March 1758. [SM.20.161]

**BRODERICK, CHARLES,** DD, Archbishop of Cashel, Primate of Munster, and Bishop of Emly, died in Rutland Square, Dublin, on 6 May 1822. [SM.90.269]

**BROOKE, HENRY VAUGHAN,** aged 65, for 36 years a Member of Parliament for County Donegal, died in London on 28 November 1807. [SM.69.959]

**BROUGHAM, Reverend HENRY,** married Catherine Anne Mona Macartney, youngest daughter of the late Sir John Macartney of Lish, County Armagh, in Dublin on 16 March 1826. [SM.97.766]

**BROW, JOHN,** of Tinnede, aged 109, died in County Dublin on 28 January 1761. [SM.23.111]

**BROWN, CHARLES,** a book-seller, died in Dublin on 3 July 1807. [SM.69.718]

**BROWN, JAMES,** aged 68, a tanner, died in Belfast on 26 December 1804. [SM.67.77]

**BROWN, JAMES,** from Edinburgh, married Martha Hill, daughter of the late George Hill a merchant in Dublin, in St Mark's church, Dublin on 27 November 1823. [SM.93.767]

**BROWN, Dr JEMMET,** Archbishop of Tuam, died in Dublin on 9 June 1782. [SM.44.334]

**BROWN, JOHN,** Lieutenant Colonel of the marine forces, died in Cork on 10 February 1781. [SM.43.110]

**BROWN, ........,** son of Captain Brown of the 48th Regiment of Foot, was born in the house of Charles Crymble in Ballyclare on 12 March 1790. [SM.52.153]

**BROWNE, Dr ARTHUR,** Prime Serjeant of Ireland, died in Dublin on 8 June 1805. [SM.67.487]

**BROWNE, HENRY,** aged 90, died in Dublin in June 1790. He was uncle to the Marchioness of Buckingham and father to the lady of General O'Donnell. [SM.52.311]

**BROWNE, Mrs HONORA,** aged 102, died at Rathehill, County Limerick, on 4 January 1776. Mother of General Browne now in Riga. [SM.38.53]

**BROWNE, JAMES,** H.M. Prime serjeant at law, MP for Castlebar, and uncle to the Earl of Altamont, died in West Port on 22 October 1790. [SM.52.569]

**BROWNE, VALENTINE,** Earl of Kenmure, Viscount and Baron Castlerosse, died at Castlerosse, County Kerry, on 3 October 1812. He was succeeded in title and possessions by his eldest son Lord Castlerosse. [SM.74.807]

**BROWNLOW, ELISABETH,** daughter of William Brownlow, married the Earl of Darnley, in Lurgan in August 1791. [SM.53.466]

**BROWNLOW, WILLIAM,** formerly Member of Parliament for County Armagh, died in Richmond on 10 July 1815. [SM.77.719]

**BOYNE, Lord Viscount,** died in Dublin in April 1746. [SM.8.250]

**BRUCE, Major ISAAC,** of Sir John Bruce-Hope's Regiment of Foot, died in Dublin on 8 July 1746. [SM.8.349]

**BRYANS, PETER,** aged 117, died in the parish of Tynan, County Tyrone, on 17 February 1755. [SM.17.108]

**BRYDON, Reverend GEORGE,** aged 70, for 40 years the Presbyterian minister of Kircubbin, died in Duneveley in 1817. [SM.80.196]

**BUCHANAN, ROBERT,** Captain of the brig Hawke of Maryport, brother of the Reverend Claudius Buchanan, died in Belfast in 1811. [SM.73.720]

**BUCHANAN, ......,** daughter of Major Buchanan, was born in Limerick, in 1796. [SM.58.145]

**BUCHY, Mrs,** aged 103, died in Ireland on 16 August 1775. [SM.37.462]

**BUCKINGER, MATTHEW,** aged 65, 'born without arms and legs', died in Ireland, 1739. [SM.I.375]

**Bulkeley, Lord Viscount,** of the Kingdom of Ireland, died 1739. [SM.I.140]

**Bulkeley, Viscountess Dowager,** of Ireland, married Sir Hugh Williams, a Major of the Royal Volunteers, in London in January 1761. [SM.23.53]

**BULKELEY, HENRI FRANCIS,** General Count, formerly proprietaire of the Irish Regiment of Bulkeley in the Service of the King of France, died in London, aged 64, on 21 March 1806. [AM.67.318]

**BURCHELL, ......,** daughter of Phillis Burchall aged 63, was born in Cork on 21 June 1757. 'She swore that Francis Gwynn, a man of 74, was the father of the child.' [SM.19.382]

**BURGH, Lieutenant Colonel ULYSSES,** KCB, ADC to the Duke of Wellington, married Maria Bagenal, only daughter of the late Walter Bagenal MP for County Carlow, in Carlow on 20 June 1815. [SM.77.556]

**BURGH, WALTER HUSSEY,** chief baron of Ireland, died in Armagh on 1 October 1783. [SM.45.560]

**BURKE, Miss,** daughter of Sir Thomas Burke baronet, married the Earl of Clanricard, in Marblehead, Ireland, in 1799. [SM.61.283]

**BURNET, RICHARD,** a bookseller, died in Dublin on 15 September 1805. [SM.67.728]

**BURNETT, Major General,** commanding officer of the troops in north-eastern Ireland, died in Armagh on 29 October 1817. [SM.80.500]

**BURNSIDE, Dr,** 'an eminent physician', died in Newton Stewart, County Londonderry, in 1798. [SM.60.652]

**BURROWS, Major AMBROSE,** of the Royal Hospital near Kilmainham, died 1739. [SM.2.46]

**BURSCOUGH, Dr WILLIAM,** aged 80, Bishop of Limerick, died at his seat at New Ross on 3 April 1755. [SM.17.210]

**BURTON, Sir C.,** baronet, died at Polarton, Carlow, in 1812. [SM.74.399]

**BUSHE, AMYAS,** Fort Major of Duncannon Fort, died in Kilmurry, County Kilkenny, on 14 June 1756. [SM.18.314]

**BUTLER, JAMES,** aged 94, late Duke of Ormond, died in Avignon in 1745. [SM.7.543]

**BUTLER, JAMES,** Lord Viscount Mountgarret, died in Dublin on 13 May 1749. [SM.11.253]

**BUTLER, Captain JAMES,** aged 103, related to the late Duke of Ormond, died in Lisbon on 13 July 1766. [SM.28.389]

**BUTLER, JAMES,** Titular Archbishop of Cashel, died in Thurles on 29 August 1791. [SM.53.415]

**BUTLER, JAMES,** brother to the Earl of Ormond, married Grace Louisa Staples, daughter of John Staples of Lissau, in Ballycastle on 12 October 1807. [SM.69.956]

**BUTLER, PETER,** aged 89, Lord Viscount Galmoy, Earl of Newcastle, a Peer of Ireland, died in Paris on 18 June 1740. [SM.2.291]

**BUTLER, RICHARD,** eldest son of Lord Viscount Mountgarret, married Lady Harriot Butler, daughter of the Earl of Carrick, in Ireland on 7 October 1768. [SM.30.559]

**BUTLER, RICHARD,** the Earl of Glengal, died at Cahir House, County Tipperary, on 30 January 1819. His title devolved to his eldest son Richard Butler, Lord Viscount Cahir, Member of Parliament for County Tipperary. [SM.83.286]

**BUTLER, SOMERSET HAMILTON,** Lord Ikerrin, married Miss Boyle, daughter of Henry Boyle the Speaker of the House of Commons in Ireland, in 1744. [SM.7.249]

**BUTLER, WILLIAM,** aged 107, died in Ballyready near Ross in 1790. [SM.52.517]

**BUTLER, Mrs,** relict of Captain Thomas Butler, and daughter of Dr Cuming a physician in Dublin, died at St Stephen's Green, Dublin, on 29 December 1758. [SM.21.51]

**BUTLER, ......,** heir to the late Earl of Arran, died at his seat near Kilkenny on 13 July 1766. [SM.28.389]

**BUTLER, Colonel,** aged 95, 'for many years in Imperial service and a relation of the late Duke of Ormond', died in Barcelona on 16 January 1769. [SM.31.54]

**BUTLER, Captain,** of the Clifton an Irish revenue cruiser, married Mary Campbell, daughter of the late Baillie Colin Campbell of Campbelton, there on 8 May 1808. [SM.71.397]

**BUTSON, Reverend JAMES STRANGE,** son of the Lord Bishop of Clonfert, married Hessy Sinclair, daughter of the late William Sinclair, in Belfast on 19 June 1810. [SM.72.558]

**BYRNE, MICHAEL,** died in Ireland on 9 November 1772. [SM.34.639]

**BYRNE, ......,** three sons and two daughters of ... Byrne, were born at New Inn near Clancurry on 13/14/15 April 1753. [SM.15.205]

**BYRNE, ROGER,** aged 54, died in Ossory, in 1787, and was buried in Rosenallis, Queen's County. 'the largest person ever known in Ireland.....the coffin weighed 46 stone and was borne by 30 strong men'. [SM.49.259]

**BYRNE, THADY,** aged 104, died at Killileagh near Armagh in 1789. [SM.51.518]

**CADDEL, JOHN,** an attorney at law in Belfast, married Miss Caddel in Portaferry on 3 October 1803. [SM.65.737]

**Cahier, Lord,** of the Kingdom of Ireland, died in France in 1788. [SM.50.311]

**Caher, Lord,** married Miss Jeffries, niece to the Lord Chancellor, in Ireland in 1793. [SM.55.412]

**CAIRNS, Mrs,** aged 66, died in Ballywalter on 2 August 1817, relict of surgeon Cairns of Donaghadee, and last surviving daughter of Captain Arthur Lusk who circumnavigated the world with Lord Anson. [SM.80.99]

**CALDWELL, Sir JAMES,** died at his seat at Bellashaney on 28 January 1752. 'He has left his estate to his only daughter; and the title of baronet goes to Dr William

Caldwell, son of Colonel William Caldwell of Greenhall, brother of the gentleman now deceased, and of Sir Harry Caldwell of Bellicke.' [SM.14.101]

**CALDWELL, ANNE,** wife of George Cockburn, died in Dublin on 26 April 1769. [SM.31.279]

**CALDWELL, DAVID,** aged 103, died in Waterford on 1 April 1776. [SM.38.221]

**CALLAGHAN, .....,** son of John Callaghan, was born at Sunday's Well, Ireland, on 21 October 1769. John, the father, was 70, and his wife 60. [SM.31.558]

**CAMERON, Sergeant ALEXANDER,** pipe-major of the 92nd [Cameron Highlanders] Regiment, died in Belfast on 18 October 1817. [SM.80.399]

**CAMPBELL, ALEXANDER,** died in Dublin in 1808. [SM.70.879]

**CAMPBELL, ALEXANDER,** of Achnacroish, a Captain in the Scots Greys, married Henrietta Florence Gunne Bell, third daughter of Henry Gunne Bell, at Belvedere Place, Dublin, on 3 May 1810. [SM.72.399]

**CAMPBELL, BEAUJOLIS,** third daughter of the late Colonel Shawfield and niece of the Duke of Argyll, married Viscount Tullamore, only son of the Earl of Charleville, in Florence on 26 February 1821. [SM.87.493]

**CAMPBELL, COLIN,** a Captain of Lord John Murray's Highland Regiment, died in Dublin on 24 January 1756. [SM.18.51]

**CAMPBELL, DOUGAL,** surgeon to the 2nd Battalion of the Warwick Militia, married Miss Moore, eldest daughter of the late James Moore of Bellydivity, in Belfast in 1803. [SM.65.883]

**CAMPBELL, DUNCAN,** of Sunderland in the island of Islay, Argyll, died at Castleton, near Strabane, on 11 April 1755. He was descended from the house of Calder a second branch of the family of Argyle. [SM.17.210]

**CAMPBELL, J.,** Captain of the 12th Regiment of Foot, married Anne Saxton, only daughter of the late J. Saxton of Limerick, in St George's Church, Limerick, in 1819. [SM.83.285]

**CAMPBELL, JAMES,** of Craignish, paymaster of the 72nd Regiment, died in Limerick 'a few hours after his wife was delivered of her ninth child', on 12 December 1812. [SM.75.80]

**CAMPBELL, JOHN,** aged over 120, died in Dungannon in 1791. 'He was a soldier at the Siege of Derry'. [SM.53.570]

**CAMPBELL, Lieutenant Colonel JOHN,** of the 2nd Royal Veteran Battalion, died in Dublin on 19 June 1821. [SM.88.191]

**CAMPBELL, JOHN,** Chief Officer of Police, died at Tallow, County Waterford, on 22 December 1824. [SM.95.768]

**CAMPBELL, ROBERT,** 'one of the oldest and best established bleacher in the north of Ireland', died in Newton Limnavady, County Londonderry, in May 1807. [SM.69.479]

**CAMPBELL, WILLIAM,** an engineer, married Maria Oliver Baillie, only daughter of James Baillie of Sandymount, in Dublin in 1806. [SM.67.485]

**CAMPBELL, Reverend Dr.,** minister of the Dissenters in Clonmell for 20 years, died there on 1805. [SM.67.967]

**CAMPBELL, Mrs,** relict of Colin Campbell, Captain of the 42$^{nd}$ [Royal Highland] Regiment of Foot, died in Limerick in June 1807. [SM.69.639]

**CAMPBELL, Mr,** from Thurso, married Miss Nichol from Thurso, in Belfast on 14 December 1808. [SM.71.77]

**CAMPBELL, ........,** son of Dougal Campbell of the Royal Artillery, was born at Island Bridge, Ireland, on 7 October 1811. [S,.73.875]

**CAMPBELL, Mrs,** wife of Major Campbell of the Argyll Militia, died in Galway in 1813. [SM.75.317]

**CAMPION, Mrs BANE,** aged 108, died in Cork in 1791. [SM.53.49]

**CARBERY, Lord,** an Irish peer, died at his seat at Carass, County Limerick, on 25 August 1749. [SM.11.462]

**CARBERRY, Lady,** died in Dublin on 6 January 1806. [SM.67.79]

**CARBERRY, Lord,** died in Dublin on 4 March 1807. [SM.69.238]

**CARDEN, Sir JOHN CRAVEN,** aged 63, died at the Priory, near Templemore, on 22 November 1820. [SM.87.95]

**CARELLAN, OWEN,** aged 127, a laborer, died in Dulack, County Meath, in October 1764. [SM.26.631]

**CARLILE, Reverend JAMES,** of the Scots Church, Mary's Abbey, married Jane Wren, youngest daughter of William Wren in Kendal, in Dublin in 1821. [SM.87.294]

**Carlisle, ......,** son of the Earl of Carlisle, was born in Dublin Castle on 25 December 1781. [SM.44.54]

**Carlow, Lord Viscount HENRY,** aged 67, died in Swadlinbar, Ireland, on 22 August 1779. [SM.41.455]

**CARMICHAEL, ANDREW,** aged over 90, died at Dungannon in November 1758. 'He descended from an ancient Scotch family'. [SM.20.660]

**CARMICHAEL, Dr WILLIAM,** Archbishop of Dublin, died in Bath on 15 December 1765. 'He was brother to the Earl of Hyndford and was translated to the see of Dublin in June last, upon the death of Dr Cobbe.' [SM.27.671]

**CARPENDALE, Reverend THOMAS,** Principal of the Endowed School of Armagh, died in Armagh on 28 October 1817. [SM.80.500]

**CARPENTER, the Right Reverend,** titular Archbishop of Dublin, died in his house on Usher's Island on 29 October 1786. [SM.48.569]

**CARR, Dr CHARLES,** Bishop of Kildare, died 1739. [SM.2.46]

**Carrick, ....,** a daughter of the Earl of Carrick, was born in Dublin, on 23 January 1749. [SM.11.53]

**Carrick, ....,** son and a daughter of the Earl of Carrick, were born at Killyon, County Kilkenny, on 15 August 1750. [SM.12.398]

**Carrington, Viscount Dowager,** of Ireland, died in Whitehall on 11 May 1748. [SM.10.250]

**CARRMAN, ....,** a widow, aged 122, died in Fethard, Ireland, in January 1771. [SM.33.109]

**CARTON, Mrs JULIA,** widow of Thomas Carton, of Maidstown, County Dublin, married Lord Lecale, in 1808. [SM.70.637]

**CARY, Lady JEAN,** wife of Edward Cary and eldest sister of the Marquis of Waterford, died in Dublin on 11 December 1792. [SM.54.622]

**CARY, Dr MORDECAI,** Bishop of Killala and Athonry, died at Killala in 1751. [SM.13.502]

**Carysfort, Lord JOHN,** a Privy Councillor of Ireland, died in Lisle on 31 September 1772. [SM.34.517]

**Cassan, ......,** son and heir of Lord Cassan, was born at Cassan Park, County Wexford, in 1810. [SM.72.876]

**Castlecomer, ......,** son and heir apparent of Viscount Castlecomer, was born in Dublin on 23 April 1753. [SM.15.205]

**Castlecomer, .......,**daughter of Lord Viscount Castlecomer, was born in London in June 1754. [SM.16.308]

**Castlecomer,......, Lady Dowager,** died in Dublin on 2 September 1757. [SM.19.495]

**Castlestewart, .....,** son of the Earl of Castlestewart, was born in Dublin on 24 June 1812. [SM.74.304]

**Castlestuart, ........,** daughter of the Earl of Castlestuart, was born at Stuart Hall, County Tyrone, on 5 July 1819. [SM.84.197]

**CATHCART, HUGH,** married Miss Heatly, in Dublin, 1808. [SM.71.77]

**CAULFIELD, HENRY,** of Hockley Lodge, County Armagh, only brother of the Earl of Charlemont, married Elizabeth Margaret Browne, second daughter of Dodwell Browne of Rabines, County Mayo, granddaughter of Sir Neal O'Donnel, baronet, deceased, and niece of Lady Molyneax of Castle Dillon, County Armagh, on 30 August 1819. [SM.84.388]

**CAULFIELD, JAMES,** aged 17, second son of the Earl of Charlemont, died in Dublin on 11 September 1793. [SM.55.517]

**Cavan, RICHARD Earl of,** aged 76, died in Lamberton, Queen's County, 1742. [SM.4.142]

**Cavan, the Earl of,** married Miss Wall, daughter of James Wall in Dublin, there on 31 March 1742. [SM.4.194]

**Cavan, the Countess Dowager of,** aged 89, died in Dublin on 27 January 1743. [SM.5.102]

**Cavan, the Countess of,** died in Dublin in October 1766. [SM.28.558]

**Cavan, .......,** daughter of the Earl of Cavan, was born on 16 April 1775. [SM.37.222]

**Cavan, the Earl of,** married Miss Gould, youngest daughter of Sir Henry Gould one of the judges of the court of Common Pleas, on 8 July 1782. [SM.44.390]

**Cavan, the Countess of,** died in London on 15 April 1788. [SM.50.206]

**Cavan, .....,** son of the Earl of Cavan, was born at Eagleshurst on 26 August 1822. [SM.89.519]

**CAVENDISH, Sir HENRY,** baronet, Receiver General of Ireland, died at Frescati near Dublin on 3 August 1804. [SM.66.647]

**CHALMER, WILLIAM,** son of the late William Chalmer of Dalry a surgeon in Edinburgh, died in Cork on 27 October 1821. [SM.88.620]

**CHAMBAUD, LEWIS,** author and teacher of the French language, died in Dublin on 22 September 1776. [SM.38.510]

**CHAMBERLAIN, Mrs,** widow of Michael Chamberlain a Counsellor at Law in Dublin, died in Edinburgh on 15 May 1789. [SM.51.259]

**CHAPMAN, THOMAS,** a mariner, died in Waterford in 1796. 'He sailed round the world in HMS Centurion commanded by Commodore Anson'. [SM.58.577]

**Charlemount, the Earl of,** married Miss Hickman in Ireland in July 1768. [SM.30.389]

**Charlemount, ......., ** son of the Earl of Charlemount, was born in Ireland in February 1769. [SM.31.110]

**CHARTRES, Captain WILLIAM,** late of Handisyd's regiment, died in Ireland on his way to Scotland, on 24 October 1762. [SM.24,623]

**CHASE, JOSHUA,** aged 90, married Miss Mary Woodhouse, aged 15, at Gorey in County Wicklow in May 1767. [SM.29.334]

**CHETWYND, Mrs DEBORAH,** sister to the late and aunt to the present Lord Viscount Chetwynd of the Kingdom of Ireland, seamstress and laundress to her Majesty, died on 4 October 1788. [SM.50.569]

**CHETWYND, WILLIAM,** Viscount Chetwynd of Ireland, died on 4 April 1770. [SM.32.229]

**CHETWYND, WILLIAM,** fourth Lord Chetwynd, born 1753, died in Dennybrook near Dublin in 1791. [SM.53.570]

**CHICHESTER, ARTHUR,** Earl of Donegal, died at Marbury Hall, Cheshire, on 28 September 1757. [SM.19.557]

**CHINERY, Dr GEORGE,** Bishop of Cloyne, died there on 17 August 1780. [SM.42.447]

**CHIP, Captain,** aged 88, died at Cork on 5 July 1755. 'He came to that place from Hamburg in an open boat, with only one boy with him; he went to the West Indies with two men only; and he performed many such astonishing voyages'. [SM.17.366]

**CHUMP, JOHN,** aged 120, died in Kildare on 2 October 1769. [SM.31.558]

**Clanbrasil, HENRIETTA, Countess Dowager,** died at her seat of Templeogue, Ireland, on 10 June 1792. [SM.53.311]

**Clanmorris, Lord Baron,** aged 56, died at Newbrook, County Mayo, on 4 May 1821. [SM.87.591]

**Clanricard, the Earl of,** married Miss Vincent, youngest daughter of Sir Henry Vincent, 1740. [SM.2.338]

**Clanricard, .....,** daughter of the Earl of Clanricard, was born in January 1800. [SM.62.71]

**Clanricard, ......,** daughter of the Earl of Clanricard, was born in Portumna Castle on 25 September 1807. [SM.70.77]

**Clanricard, JOHN THOMAS, Earl of,** a General in the army, Colonel of the 60^th Regiment, Governor of Hull, and Custos Rotulorum of County Galway, died in Dublin on 27 July 1808. [SM.70.639]

**CLARKE, ISABELLA,** youngest daughter of Dr Clarke of Rutland Square, died in Dublin on 2 October 1811. [SM.73.800]

**CLAYTON, Dr ROBERT,** Bishop of Clogher, died at St Stephen's Green, Dublin, on 25 February 1758. [SM.20.110]

**CLEGHORN, GEORGE,** aged 75, Professor of Anatomy in the University of Dublin, died at his country seat in County Meath on 22 December 1789. [SM.52.50]

**CLEMENT-KENNEDY, ROBERT,** died at his seat in County Longford on 30 November 1761. 'He was lineally descended from the great Bryan Borama or Boro, O'Kennedy, sole king of Ireland in the year 1002'. [SM.23.671]

**Clonbrock, Lord,** of the Kingdom of Ireland, and a member of the Privy Council of that island, died at his seat of Clonbrock on 23 August 1795. [SM.57.546]

**Cloncarty, the Countess Dowager,** of Ireland, died in London on 14 January 1759. [SM.21.51]

**Clonmell, the Earl of,** married Lady Harriet Greville, second daughter of the Earl of Warwick, on 9 February 1805. [SM.67.158]

**Clonmell, ........,** daughter of the Earl of Clonmell was born on 6 November 1812. [SM.74.966]

**Clonmell, ........,** twin daughters of the Earl of Clonmell, were born on 1 February 1820. [SM.85.290]

**CLOTWORTHY, ....., Earl** of Massarene, aged 62, died in Antrim Castle on 5 March 1805. [SM.67.237]

**Cloyne, the Bishop of,** married Miss Benson, in Dublin in December 1776. [SM.38.677]

**CLUNE, Lieutenant,** of the 63$^{rd}$ Regiment, married Miss Boyd, daughter of Captain Boyd of the same regiment, in Belfast in 1803. [SM.65.883]

**COAPLAND, Mrs,** aged 121, died in Sligo on 10 January 1807. 'She married a serjeant in the Royal Irish Dragoons 80 years ago'. [SM.69.79]

**COBBE, Dr CHARLES,** aged 79, Archbishop of Dublin, died there on 14 April 1764. [SM.27.223]

**COCKBURN, Sir JAMES,** baronet, Lieutenant Colonel of the 48$^{th}$ Regiment of Foot, died at Bandon on 13 March 1780. [SM.42.167]

**COCKBURN, Lady,** widow of Sir James Cockburn baronet, died in Bandon in 1798. [SM.60.214]

**COEN, MARY,** aged 112, died in Ireland on 29 December 1775. [SM.38.53]

**COLE, Reverend WILLIAM MONTGOMERY,** Dean of Waterford, third son of the late Earl of Enniskillen, died in Enniskillen in August 1804. [SM.66.728]

**COLE, Mrs,** sister to the Earl of Enniskillen, died at the Black Rock near Dublin in 1792. [SM.53.361]

**Colerain, the Earl of,** died in 1794. 'He is succeeded by his brother the Hon. Major Hanger'. [SM.57.68]

**COLTHURST, Sir JOHN CONWAY,** baronet, died in Old Connaught, near Bray in Ireland, on 19 January 1787. [SM.49.102]

**COLTHURST, Sir NICHOLAS CONWAY,** baronet, married Harriet Larouche, daughter of David Larouche, in Dublin on 21 April 1788. [SM.50.256]

**COLLIER, ........,** aged 137, died in Ireland during January 1750. [SM.12.54]

**COLLIN, DENNIS,** aged 116, 'a peasant on the Trabolgan demesne', died in 1823. [SM.91.776]

**COLVILLE, Lieutenant Colonel,** aged 71, Commandant of the Royal Hibernian Military School, Phoenix Park, Dublin, died on 3 April 1818. [SM.81.499]

**CONDON, .....,** aged 105, a skinner, died in Dublin in November 1771. [SM.33.671]

**CONNOR, EDWARD,** aged 122, died in Taylorstown, County Wicklow, in 1815. [SM.77.959]

**CONNOR, Mr J.,** died in Tralee in 1803. [SM.65.739]

**CONOLLY, DANIEL,** born in Oldcastle, Ireland, on 17 March 1738, a soldier at the sieges of Louisbourg and of Quebec, fought at Martinico and Havannah, later Treasurer of Crail, Fife, died in Anstruther, Fife, on 22 March 1818. [SM.81.499]

**CONOLLY, Lady LOUISA,** aged 77, sister of the late Duke of Richmond and relict of the late Thomas Conolly, died in Castletown House, County Kildare, on 26 July 1821. [SM.88.295]

**CONOLLY, THOMAS,** of Castletown, County Kildare, married Lady Louisa Lennox, third daughter of the late Duke of Richmond and sister to the Countess of Kildare, at Curton, Ireland, the seat of the Earl of Kildare, on 30 December 1758. [SM.21.51]

**CONOLLY, WILLIAM,** a Privy Councillor and a member of the House of Commons in Ireland, died in Dublin on 2 January 1757. [SM.16.50]

**CONNOLLY, Mr,** aged 107, died in Dublin on 19 April 1768. [SM.30.223]

**CONNELLY ,......,** aged 118, died near Edinderry, Ireland, in 1794. 'He remembered the landing of King William and the Battle of the Boyne'. [SM.56.412]

**CONYNGHAM, HENRY,** Viscount Conyngham and Baron Mount Charles in the Kingdom of Ireland, a Privy Councillor and Lord Lieutenant of County Londonderry, died in Bath on 3 April 1781. [SM.43.223]

**CONYNGHAM, WILLIAM BURTON,** a Commissioner for executing the office of Lord High Treasurer in Ireland, died in Dublin in 1796. [SM.58.432]

**COOROBEE, DENNIS,** of Balladangan, aged 117, died in Arkenny, County Galway, in 1804. 'he was married 7 times, and when married last he was 93 years old; by his wives he had 48 children, 236 grandchildren, 944 great grandchildren, and 25 great great grand-children'. [SM.67.75]

**COOTE, CHARLES HENRY,** aged 28, Lieutenant Colonel of the Queen's County Militia, died in Leopardstown on 5 August 1810. [SM.72.798]

**COOTE, RICHARD,** Earl of Bellamont in the Kingdom of Ireland, died in Birchmorton, Worcestershire, on 3 February 1766. [SM.28.55]

**COPE, Dr HENRY,** State Physician, died in Dublin, 1743. [SM.5.102]

**CORBET, FRANCIS,** DD, Dean of St Patrick's in Dublin, died there on 24 August 1775, aged 92. [SM.37.463]

**CORBET, ROBERT,** of Corbethall, County Wexford, Captain of the Aberdeenshire Militia, died in Edinburgh on 27 May 1804, and was buried in Greyfriars Churchyard. [SM.66.566]

**Cork, Earl of,** married Miss Courtenay, niece to the Earl of Sandwich, on 31 August 1764. [SM.26.463]

**Cork, .....,** son and heir of the Earl of Cork, was born in London on 17 May 1765. [SM.27.279]

**Cork, ......,** daughter of the Earl of Cork, was born in London on 10 August 1766. [SM.28.446]

**Cork, ......,** daughter of the Earl of Cork, was born in London on 7 October 1806 [SM.67.806]

**CORNIELLE, DANIEL,** married Miss Stewart, daughter of Charles Ross Stewart of the East India Company Service, in Dublin in 1796. [SM.58.432]

**CORRY, ARMAR LOWRY,** Member of Parliament for County Tyrone, married Lady Harriot Hobart, eldest daughter of the Earl of Buckinghamshire, Lord Lieutenant of Ireland, in Dublin Castle in March 1780. [SM.42.166]

**CORRY, ISAAC,** aged 86, of Newry, died in Belfast in 1809. [SM.71.720]

**CORRY, ISAAC,** aged 61, a trustee of the Linen Board, born in Newry, died in Dublin on 15 April 1813. [SM.75.478]

**CORSCADEN, ROBERT,** of Londonderry, married Helen Findlator, eldest daughter of the late John

Findlator of Greenock, there on 22 January 1821. [SM.87.189]

**CORY, JAMES,** Secretary to the Linen Board and Clerk of the Journals of the Irish House of Commons, died in Dublin on 25 November 1795. [SM.57.818]

**COSTELLO, MARY,** aged 102, died at Countess's Bush, County Kilkenny, on 12 June 1824. 'Her mother Matilda Pickman aged 102, her grandmother died at 120, and her great grandmother exceeded 125 years. Mary Costello's brother lived to over 100 years'. [SM.94.255]

**COTTEREL, Dr,** Bishop of Leighlin and Ferns in Ireland, died on 21 June 1744. [SM.6.298]

**COULSON, HENRY,** a Master of the Irish Court of Chancery, married Elizabeth, Lady Dowager Tracton, relict of James, Lord Tracton, Chief Baron of the Exchequer, in Dublin on 4 August 1792. [SM.53.412]

**COURSE, JOHN,** aged 112, died in Calvintown, County Kildare, on 18 August 1752. 'He was born in Languedoc, France, bred a Protestant, served in the French Army, later in Dutch service, to Ireland under the Duke of Schomberg, enlisted under King William, fought against King James, then took up farming.' [SM.14.415]

**COWAN, DAVID,** of the 93rd Highlanders, married Sarah Anne Campbell, daughter of the late Colonel Campbell, at Kildeeran church, County Tipperary, on 24 September 1817. [SM.80.294]

**COWAN, MOSES JACOB,** aged 65, 'the little Polander', two and a half feet high, born in Polish Prussia, died in Dublin on 16 February 1748. [SM.10.102]

**COX, Dr MICHAEL,** Archbishop of Cashel, died in Ireland 'at a very advanced age' on 2 June 1779. [SM.41.341]

**COX, THOMAS,** formerly a Lieutenant in General Browne's Horse, died at Newbrook, County Galway, on 12 May 1759. 'at the battle of Preston in 1745 he lost his right leg and had the other miserably mangled'. [SM.21.273]

**CRADOCK, Dr JOHN,** Archbishop of Dublin and Primate of All Ireland, died at the palace in Kevin's Street, Dublin, on 11 December 1778. [SM.40.686]

**CRAIG, CHARLES,** from Londonderry, died in Tobago in 1811. [SM.73.800]

**CRAWFORD, HENRY,** aged 81, formerly a Captain of Dragoons, died in Dublin on 7 September 1757. 'He served in part of King William's and all of Queen Anne's wars'. [SM.19.495]

**CRAWFORD, Councillor,** of Dublin, married Mrs Barry, the celebrated actress, in July 1778. [SM.40.389]

**CRAWFORD, Lieutenant,** of the Elgin Fencibles, married Miss English of Littlebridge, County Waterford, on 4 October 1798. [SM.60.729]

**CRAWFORD, ......,** son of Arthur Crawford, was born in Belfast on 28 April 1811. [SM.73.397]

**CRAWFORD, Mrs,** relict of Archibald Crawford a merchant in Leith, and mother of Major Wilkie of the 38th Regiment and Lieutenant Crawford of the 60th Regiment, died in Downpatrick on 22 September 1815. [SM.77.875]

**CRAWLEY, MARGARET,** born in Dundalk in 1688, 'had been abroad in all Queen Anne's wars as keeper of a suttling booth in the camps. She had, for many years past, let out lodgings to poor people, and is said to have died worth near £2000 the greatest part of which she has left to a blacksmith. She had been married to nine husbands, but never had any issue.' [SM.27.391]

**CREIGHTON, ABRAHAM,** Lord Erme of Crum Castle, County Fermanagh, died in Dublin on 2 June 1772. [SM.34.333]

**CREMORNE, Lord Baron,** married Miss Whaley from Dublin, at Ematrus, County Monaghan, on 10 April 1815. [SM.77.398]

**CROFTON, Sir MALBY,** died at his seat in County Sligo on 29 February 1808. 'he served under the immortal Wolfe at the siege of Quebec'. [SM.70.239]

**CROFTON, WILLIAM GEORGIUS,** aged 26, Lieutenant Captain of the Coldstream Guards, fourth son of Baroness Crofton of Moat Park, County Roscommon, died in France from a wound received at Bayonne, in 1814. [SM.76.640]

**CROKER, JOHN,** late Surveyor General of Ireland and father to the Secretary of the Admiralty, died on 30 April 1814. [SM.76.559]

**CROMIE, Miss,** eldest daughter of William Cromie in Ireland, married Colonel Forbes of the 11th Regiment of Foot, on 11 November 1773. [SM.35.516]

**CROOKSHANK, ALEXANDER,** died in Dublin on 10 December 1813. He was succeeded by his son George Crookshank. [SM.76.153]

**CROSBIE, Lord Viscount,** son of the Earl of Glandore in Ireland, married Miss Sackville, daughter of Lord George Germaine, in London on 26 November 1777. [SM.39.622]

**CROSBIE, WILLIAM,** Earl of Glandoe, a Privy Councillor of Ireland, aged 66, died in Dublin on 11 May 1781. 'He has left issue of 1 son and 3 daughters'. [SM.43.279]

**CROSS, ABRAHAM,** died on Nyrl's Quay, Cork, in 1804. [SM.66.479]

**CUFFE, ORWAY,** Earl of Desart, 'one of the Irish representative peers in the Imperial Parliament', died in Dublin on 3 August 1804. [SM.66.647]

**CUFFE, Lieutenant Colonel,** of the 13th Light Dragoons, brother of Lord Dysart and Member of Parliament for Kilkenny, died in Athlone in 1792. [SM.53.519]

**CUNNINGHAM, ALEXANDER,** 'a very eminent surgeon in Dublin', died in Meath Hospital, Dublin, on 27 August 1781. [SM.43.503]

**CUNNINGHAM, SAMUEL,** Captain of Jordan's Regiment of Foot, died in Limerick on 28 December 1753. [SM.15.628]

**CUNNINGHAM, THOMAS,** Captain of the 45th Regiment of Foot, son of the late William Cunninghame of Lainshaw, died in Dublin on 1 December 1805. [SM.67.967]

**CUNNINGHAM, WILLIAM,** of Dromona, Ireland, married Helen Shiels, eldest daughter of the late Daniel Shiels of the Royal Navy, at Hermitage Place, Leith, on 18 September 1822. [SM.90.520]

**CUNNINGHAM, .....,** daughter of William Cunningham, was born in Dromona, County Antrim, on 13 August 1823. [SM.92.382]

**CURRIE, JOHN,** Captain of the 47th Regiment, son of the late James Currie of Braidkirk, died in Cork on 17 May 1806. [SM.67.486]

**CURTIN, Reverend PATRICK,** aged 101, parish priest of Dysart, died in Ireland in 1790. [SM.52.311]

**CUSSE, JOHN,** Lord Baron of Desert, an Irish peer, died in Dublin on 26 June 1749. [SM.11.302]

**CUTHBERT, JOHN,** aged 62, Surveyor General of Customs, died in Coleraine on 12 August 1818. [SM.82.296]

**D'AGAR, Mrs,** aged 106, died in Dublin in July 1756. [SM.18.416]

**DALY, ARTHUR HENRY,** of Galway, nephew of the Earl of Aran, Marquis of Clanricard, married Miss Ogle, second daughter of General Ogle, late of Cawsey Park, Northumberland, in 1791. [SM.53.152]

**DALY, DENIS,** Member of Parliament for County Galway, Muster Master General of the forces in Ireland, and a Privy Councillor, died in Dunsandle, County Galway, in 1791. [SM.53.570]

**DALY, MICHAEL,** nephew of the Earl of Clanricard, married Miss Doyne, daughter of the Earl of Arran, in Dublin in February 1766. [SM.28.111]

**DALY, Mrs,** 'wife of a comber and weaver, a son, the day after of another, and the day following of a daughter, who, with the mother are likely to do well. It is remarkable, that this woman was last year delivered of the same number, and within three years has had three children'. [SM.30.278]

**DALY, Mrs,** wife of Arthur H. Daly, daughter of Paul Gore, cousin of the Marquis of Abercorn and of the Earl of Arran, died at Loughrea on 15 February 1812. [SM.74.239]

**DALY, ......,** three daughters of Timothy Daly, a laborer, were born in Gartnalaby, Dunbollig parish, County Cork, on 17 August 1823. [SM.92.510]

**DARLINGTON, ROBERT,** married Ellen Folds, daughter of William Folds of Great Strand Street, in St Mary's Church, Dublin, on 11 October 1823. [SM.92.639]

**Darnley, ......,** son of the Earl of Darnley, was born in Dublin on 30 June 1767. [SM.29.389]

**DASTIFF, JUDITH,** aged 109, died at the Inn's Quay Infirmary, Dublin, on 17 December 1756. 'Her death was occasioned by a brewer's dray running over her.' [SM.18.627]

**DAVENPORT, ANNA MARIA,** only daughter of the late William Davenport in Londonderry, married William Galloway, a merchant in Edinburgh, in Dundee on 16 August 1808. [SM.70.637]

**DAVENPORT, WILLIAM,** married Mrs Wilson, in Londonderry on 17 March 1811. [SM.73.316]

**DAVIDSON, JAMES,** teacher at Dalmeny Grammar School, died in Dublin on 25 August 1791. [SM.53.414]

**DEAN, WILLIAM,** LL.D., and a member of the Royal Irish Academy, died in Dublin in 1793. [SM.55.620]

**DEANE, Sir ROBERT,** a Privy Councillor and Member of Parliament for Carrie's Fort in County Wicklow, died in Dublin on 7 February 1770. [SM.32.111]

**DEANE, T. F.,** Colonel of the 38th Regiment, eldest son of Lord Muskery, married ..... Haynes, second daughter of M. Haynes of Bishop's Castle, Shropshire, in Kinsale on 10 January 1815. [SM.77.236]

**DE BLAQUIERE, Lord,** a Knight of the Bath and a baronet, died at Bray near Dublin on 27 August 1812. He was succeeded in titles and estates by his eldest son John a prisoner in France. [SM.74.805]

**DE COURCY, GERALD,** 24th Baron of Kinsale, died in Kinsale on 1 December 1759. [SM.21.663]

**DE COURCY, JOHN,** Baron of Kinsale, died in Kinsale on 17 March 1776. [SM.38.163]

**DE COURCY, JOHN,** Lord Kinsale, Baron Courcy, and Baron of Ringrone, died in Cork in 1822. [SM.90.270]

**DE COURCY, Reverend GERALD,** brother to Lord Kinsale, died in Kinsale on 17 May 1792. [SM.53.250]

**DE COURCY, Miss,** daughter of Lord Kinsale, married Captain Andrew Agnes of the 12th Regiment of Foot, in Kinsale on 18 May 1792. [SM.53.309]

**DE COURCY, Governor,** brother to the late Lord Kinsale, died in Kinsale on 15 January 1824. [SM.93.256]

**DEDWICH, Reverend Dr,** aged 84, died in Dublin in 1823. He was the author of 'Antiquities of Ireland' and a member of many of the learned societies in Europe. [SM.92.512]

**DE GRANGUES, Lieutenant General HENRY,** Colonel of a regiment of horse, and a Major General on the Irish Establishment, died at Newland, County Dublin, on 23 June 1754. [SM.16.308]

**DE HAROLD, Baron,** a General in Bavarian service, died in Dusseldorf in 1808. 'This gentleman was of a very old and respectable family in the south of Ireland'. [SM.70.719]

**DE JEAN, Lieutenant General LOUIS,** aged 85, Major General on the Irish staff, Colonel of Caribiniers, 3$^{rd}$ Regiment of Horse, died in Dublin on 24 September 1764. [SM.26.519]

**DE LA BOUCHETIERE, Mrs MARGARET,** daughter of the late Charles de la Bouchetiere, Colonel of Dragoons on the Irish Establishment, died at her lodgings in Cuffe Street, Dublin, in 1787 or 1788. 'She was born during 1696 in Ghent during the Flemish wars.' [SM.50.51]

**Delwin, Lord,** son of the Earl of West Meath, died in Dublin on 6 August 1761. 'He died of a wound he received in a duel fought about eight days ago with Mr Reilly.' [SM.23.447]

**De Montalto, Lord,** died in Dundrum, County Tipperary, on 26 May 1777. [SM.39.279]

**De Montmorency, Viscount Frankfort**, died at his villa near Clontarff on 21 September 1822. [SM.90.632]

**DEMPSTER, JAMES,** MD of the 93$^{rd}$ Regiment, married Elizabeth Maria Carroll, only child of John Carroll of Newland, County Tipperary, at Nenagh on 3 February 1818. [SM.81.294]

**DEMPSTER, .....,** son of James Dempster MD, was born in Ninagh on 22 January 1823. [SM.93.1824]

**DEMPSTER, .......,** son of Dr Dempster, was born in Nenagh on 25 June 1825. [SM.96.254]

**DENHAM, Dr,** aged 65, 'the celebrated Irish patriot', died in Belfast in 1820. [SM.85.488]

**De Rupe and Fermay, Viscount,** died in Dublin in January 1777. [SM.39.54]

**Desert, Lord,** an Irish peer, married Miss Thornhill in Dublin on 2 September 1752. [SM.14.462]

**Desart, the Earl of,** married Catherine O'Connor, eldest daughter of Maurice N. O'Connor, at Mount Pleasant, King's County, on 7 October 1817. [SM.80.497]

**Devenish, the Marquis of,** a native of Ireland, aged 70, a Major General in the Emperor's service, Governor of Courtray, died in Brussels, 1740. [SM.2.237]

**DEVEREAUX, Mrs JANE,** aged 110, died in Ballybouglan, King's County, in 1817. [SM.81.96]

**DEVEREAUX, Mrs,** aged 119, born in Scotland, died in the widows' house of St Michael's parish, Dublin, on 21 January 1753. [SM.15.54]

**DE VIANE, Marquis,** died in County Roscommon on 7 October 1769. [SM.31.559]

**DEWEY, WILLIAM,** aged 110, died in Kilcullen, County Kildare, in February 1778. [SM.40.111]

**DICK, SAMUEL,** a merchant, died in Dublin in 1802. [SM.64.184]

**DICK, .....,** twins, children of Lieutenant Colonel Dick of the Royal Highlanders, were born in Limerick in 1823. [SM.91.774]

**DICKENSON, Reverend B.,** minister of an Anabaptist congregation in Waterford, died there on 4 November 1810. [SM.72.959]

**DICKSON, DAVID SOMERVILLE RANALDSON,** of Blairhall, a Lieutenant of the 2$^{nd}$ [Royal North British] Dragoons, married Anna Crymble, youngest daughter of the late Charles Crymble of Ballyclare, County Antrim, in Edinburgh in 1812. [SM.74.566]

**DICKSON, HUGH,** a physician in Portaferry, died there on 16 September 1804. [SM.67.74]

**DICKSON, Reverend WILLIAM,** second son of the late Bishop of Down and Connor, married Bettina Webster, niece of the late Sir Godfrey Webster baronet, on 9 February 1805. [SM.67.158]

**DIGBY, Reverend WILLIAM,** aged 82, Dean of Clonfert, died at Mountjoy Square, Dublin, on 14 May 1812. [SM.74.567]

**DIGBY,. ......,** son of Benjamin Digby, was born in Mountjoy Square, Dublin, in 1824. [SM.93.767]

**DILKES, Lieutenant General MICHAEL O'BRIAN,** Governor of the Royal Hospital near Dublin, died 10 July 1761. [SM.23.391]

**DILKES, General MICHAEL O'BRIAN,** Colonel of the 5$^{th}$ Regiment of Foot, died in Dublin on 20 August 1775. [SM.37.463]

**Dillon, Lord,** of the Kingdom of Ireland, a Colonel in French service, died in London, 1741. [SM.3.475]

**DILLON, CHARLES,** 12th Viscount Dillon, Privy Councillor, Governor of Mayo and Roscommon, Constable of Athlone Castle, a Trustee of the Linen Manufactures, and a Knight of St Patrick, died at Loughglin on 9 November 1813. [SM.76.79]

**DILLON, JOHN,** Earl of Roscommon, died in Knockrenny on 28 August 1782. The title devolved to Charles Dillon of Kilcock. [SM.44.502]

**DILLON, Sir JOHN,** baronet, a Baron of the Holy Roman Empire, died in Lismullen, County Meath, on 17 July 1805. [SM.67.646]

**DILLON, PATRICK,** Earl of Roscommon and Baron of Kilkenny, died in Barbaravilla, County Roscommon, on 17 November 1816. He was succeeded in title by his cousin Michael Robert Dillon, son of Captain Michael Dillon late of the Dublin County Militia killed at the Battle of Ross in 1798, during the rebellion. [SM.78.959]

**DILLON, ROBERT,** titular Earl of Roscommon in Ireland, Baron of West Kilkenny, Colonel of a regiment of foot, and a Marshal in the armies of France, died in Paris on 25 March 1770. [SM.32.167]

**Dillon, Lady Viscountess,** mother of the present Viscount Dillon of the Kingdom of Ireland, died in London on 19 June 1794. [SM.56.375]

**DIVE, Major,** of the Fifeshire Fencibles, married Miss Rolleston of Carrickfergus on 12 May 1797. [SM.59.360]

**DOGGHED, PATRICK,** died in Drogheda on 3 February 1767. 'He was a drummer in King James's army at the Battle of the Boyne'. [SM.29.110]

**DOHERTY, ANTHONY,** aged 105, a blacksmith, died at Park, near Coleraine on 25 September 1825. [SM.96.639]

**DOMVILLE, COMPTON,** of Santry House, County Dublin, married Elizabeth Frances Lindsay, only daughter of the Lord Bishop of Kildare, at Glasnevin Church, Ireland, on 21 October 1811. [SM.73.877]

**DON, O'CONNOR,** 'a lineal descendant of the last Irish monarch of that name', died in Cloonalis, County Roscommon, on 21 September 1795. [SM.57.682]

**Donegal, Countess of,** died in Allinger, Surrey, on 16 June 1743. [SM.5.295]

**Donegal, ARTHUR, Earl of,** married Mrs Moore, in Bath on 25 October 1788. [SM.50.569]

**Donegal, the Countess of,** died at Fisherwick, Staffordshire, on 19 September 1789. [SM.51.466]

**Donegal, the Earl of,** aged 51, married Barbara Godfrey, aged 21, daughter of the Reverend Dr Godfrey of Belfast, in London on 12 October 1790. 'His Lordship has been married twice before, and has children as old as his Lady'. [SM.52.516]

**Donegal, ......,** son of the Marquis of Donegal, was born at Donegal House, Dublin, on 16 November 1805. [SM.67.155]

**Donegal, ......,** son of the Marquis of Donegal, was born in Ormeau, October 1808. [SM.70.878]

**Donegal, ......,** son of the Marquis of Donegal, was born in Donegal House on 12 November 1811. [SM.73.956]

**Donegal, ......,** seventh son of the Marquis of Donegal, was born in Ormeau near Belfast on 19 December 1814. [SM.77.75]

**DONELLY, DANIEL,** 'the Hibernian pugilist', died in Dublin in 1820. [SM.85.488]

**Donerayle, Lord Viscount,** married Miss Skeffington, sister to Lord Viscount Massereen, in Dublin 1739. [SM.2.46]

**Doneraile, the Viscountess,** died in Dublin on 3 December 1761. [SM.23.671]

**Doneraile, Lord Viscount,** of the Kingdom of Ireland, died in Bath on 15 April 1767. [SM.29.213]

**Doneraile, Lord Viscount,** died at his seat of Doneraile in Ireland on 22 May 1787. 'He is succeeded in title and estate by his eldest son Hayes St Leger'. [SM.49.259]

**Doneraile, Viscount,** aged 65, died in Doneraile House, County Cork, on 8 November 1819. [SM.84.584]

**DOPPING, Dr ANTHONY,** Bishop of Offory, died in Dublin on 1 February 1743. [SM.5.102]

**DORMAN, or DIERMOTT, JOHN,** died in Strabane in 1819. 'He was born at Boigh in the parish of Cloulee, County Donegal, 24 August 1709. His father was a laborer, and lived to the age of 111. His mother's name was Margaret Sharkey, she lived to be nearly 113 years old'. [SM.83.288]

**DORIAN, Reverend JAMES,** aged 27, Roman Catholic curate of Dundalk, died on 21 October 1817 of typhus. [SM.80.499]

**DOTAH, AMBROSE,** aged 111, a beggar, married Mary Stapleton, aged 94, a beggar, in Fethard, County Tipperary, in November 1767. [SM.29.614]

**DOUGLAS, WILLIAM,** MD, late surgeon to the Aberdeen Fencibles, died in Mallow on 25 January 1805. [SM.67.237]

**DOUGLAS, Lieutenant Colonel,** of the 27th Regiment of Foot, died in Dublin during 1788. [SM.50.414]

**DOUGLAS, ......,** son of Colonel Douglas of the 97th Regiment, was born in Cork in 1817. [SM.80.193]

**Down and Connor, the Bishop of,** married Miss Black from Edinburgh, in Dublin on 7 June 1766. [SM.28.335]

**Down, .....,** son of the Lord Bishop of Down, was born in Dublin in January 1805. [SM.67.158]

**DOWNE, Lord Viscount,** of Ireland, died of wounds received at the battle of Campen, 1760. [SM.22.669]

**DOWNES, Dr ROBERT,** Bishop of Raphoe, died at his house at St Stephen's Green on 6 July 1763. [SM.25.415]

**Downes, Lord,** former Chief Justice of the Court of King's Bench in Ireland, died on 2 March 1826. [SM.97.511]

**Downshire, the Marquis of,** died in Hillsborough on 7 September 1801. [SM.63.660]

**DOYLE, Lieutenant General,** died in Waterford on 12 June 1823. [SM.92.128]

**DRELINCOURT, Miss,** daughter of the late Dean of Armagh, married Lord Viscount Primrose, 1740. [SM.2.237]

**Drogheda,.....,** a daughter of the Earl of Drogheda was born 1739. [SM.I.235]

**Drogheda, the Earl of,** married Lady Anne Conway, eldest daughter of the Earl of Hertford, Lord Lieutenant of Ireland, in Ireland on 15 February 1766. [SM.28.111]

**Drogheda, .....,** son of the Earl of Drogheda, born in Ireland on 20 August 1770. [SM.32.457]

**DRUM, JAMES,** died in Trim, Ireland, in March 1751, aged above 107. [SM.13.163]

**DRUMMOND, Captain,** 'the oldest captain in the service, died at Kinsale, 1742. [SM.5.50]

**DRUMMOND, .....,** son of Lady Charlotte Drummond, was born in Cove near Cork in January 1809. [SM.71.158]

**DRUMMOND, Reverend W. H.,** minister of the Presbyterian Church of Strand Street, married Catherine Blackly, daughter of the late Robert Black of Lurgan Street, in Dublin on 27 September 1824. [SM.94.639]

**DRURY, CHARLES,** of the 3$^{rd}$ Regiment of Dragoon Guards, married Elizabeth Hart, eldest daughter of Lieutenant Colonel Hart, at St Peter's church in Dublin on 2 December 1819. [SM.85.93]

**DUDGEON, SAMUEL,** a woollen draper, died in Dublin on 4 May 1804. [SM.66.479]

**DUFF, Captain,** of the 3<sup>rd</sup> Foot Guards, married Mary Finlay, youngest daughter and co-heiress of the late William Finlay of Gunetts, in Dublin in December 1808. [SM.71.77]

**DUGGAN, ESTHER,** aged 119, died near Drumcondra on 18 May 1768. [SM.30.279]

**DUGGAN, .....,** four children were born to a washerwoman in Ballytruckle, Waterford, on 24 August 1825. [SM.96.510]

**DUGGIN, Mrs CLARE,** aged 104, born in Ireland, died in London on 15 September 1770. [SM.32.558]

**DUIGENAN, Dr,** married Mrs Heptenstal, widow of the late G. Heptenstal, attorney and solicitor to the Dublin Police, of St Andrew's Street, in Dublin in October 1807. 'The bridegroom is upwards of 70 years of age; the bride in neither young nor handsome, and has several children'. [SM.69.956]

**DUNBAR, Lieutenant General THOMAS,** Lieutenant Governor of Gibraltar, died in Dublin on 11 February 1767. [SM.29.110]

**Dunboyne, Lord,** married Miss Macnamara, in Dublin on 3 June 1773. [SM.35.335]

**Dunboyne, Lord,** died in County Meath, on 13 August 1773. [SM.25.446]

**DUNDAS, FRANCIS,** Captain of the 81<sup>st</sup> Regiment, married Miss Wallace, in Dublin in 1819. [SM.83.285]

**DUNDAS, PHILIP,** nephew of Henry Dundas, and brother to the Lord Advocate for Scotland, married Mrs Lindsay, in Dublin in 1790. [SM.52.412]

**Dunfany, Lady,** died at Dunfany Castle on 13 October 1791. [SM.53.517]

**DUNN, Mrs ALICE,** aged 102, died in Rathcoffy, County Kildare, on 11 January 1768. [SM.30.54]

**DUNN, JAMES,** an eminent farmer of Dolphin's Barn, Ireland, married Miss Mary Anne McCarty of Back Lane, aged 16, on 6 September 1768. [SM.30.502]

**DUNN, Mrs MARY,** aged 115, wife of John Dunn, died near Castlebar in 1814. [SM.76.400]

**DUNN, ......,** son of Captain Dunn of the Royal Navy, was born in Waterford on 6 October 1824. [SM.94.638]

**DU PERRON, ......,** Lieutenant Colonel of Wynyard's regiment of foot, died in Dublin on 31 August 1749. [SM.11.462]

**DWYER, JOHN,** aged 115, a husbandman, died at Ballinderry on 31 March 1763. [SM.25.301]

**DYAS, Captain,** aged 110, died in Dublin, 1741. [SM.3.94]

**EARLY, Mr.,** aged 112, died in Temple Lane, Dublin, in July 1768. 'He served in King William's army at the Siege of Derry'. [SM.30.389]

**Earlsfort, ......,** daughter of Lord Earlsfort, was born in Dublin on 14 May 1787. [SM.49.257]

**EAST, Lieutenant Colonel WILLIAM,** of Honeywood's Horse, died at the Dublin barracks on 7 August 1766. [SM.28.436]

**ECLIN, THOMAS,** died in Dublin on 24 January 1754. [SM.16.108]

**EDMONSTONE, Major CHARLES,** brother of Sir Archibald Edmonstone of Duntreath, baronet, died at North Lodge, Ireland, on 14 June 1791. [SM.53.309]

**EDWARDS, Sergeant HENRY,** aged 105, died in Glenygourland in the parish of Donaghadee, on 4 December 1813. 'He enlisted in the army at the age of 35, continued 20 years in the army, was discharged in 1763, and remained a pensioner for 50 years'. [SM.76.157]

**EDWIN, ......,** a comedian, died in Dublin on 13 February 1805. [SM.67.237]

**Egmont, the Countess of,** died in Belle Vue near Dublin on 25 January 1826. [SM.97.256]

**ELDER, Reverend HENRY,** for 32 years Presbyterian minister of the parish of Faughanvale, died at Muir, Ireland, on 24 July 1817. [SM.80.99]

**Ely, the Marquis of,** died in Dublin on 30 March 1806. He was succeeded by his son Lord Loftus, Member of Parliament for Wexford. [SM.67.319]

**Enniskillen, ......,** daughter of the Countess of Enniskillen, was born in 1811. [SM.73.635]

**ERSKINE, WILLIAM,** a Lieutenant of the 9th Regiment of Foot, died in Dublin Barracks in June 1804. [SM.66.567]

**ESKIN, MARTHA,** aged 104, died in Carnew in 1814. [SM.76.400]

**ESTE, Dr,** Bishop of Waterford, died in Dublin on 2 December 1745. [SM.7.594]

**EVANS, GEORGE,** Lord Carberry, an Irish peer, died in Ireland on 13 February 1759. [SM.21.101]

**EVANS, GEORGE,** Lord Carberry of the Kingdom of Ireland, aged 39, died in London on 31 December 1804. He married Miss Watson, daughter of Colonel Watson in 1792, but dying without issue his titles and estates devolve to his uncle John Evans in Dublin. [SM.67.77]

**EYRE, Lord JOHN,** died in Ireland on 1 October 1781. [SM.43.557]

**EYRE, STRATFORD,** Governor of Galway, died in Dublin Castle on 11 December 1767. [SM.29.670]

**EYRE, Colonel THOMAS,** MP for the borough of Fore in West Meath, died in the House of Commons, Dublin, on 22 February 1772. [SM.34.111]

**FALCONER, Alderman GEORGE,** printer of the Dublin Journal, died in Dublin on 18 August 1775. [SM.37.463]

**FALLS, JOHN,** aged 110, died in the manor of Carrick near Macquire's Bridge, Ireland, on 16 July 1754. [SM.16.357]

**FANE, Lord,** an Irish peer, died in Basseldon, Berkshire, on 7 July 1744. He was succeeded by his son Charles Fane. [SM.6.346]

**FANE, Lord Viscount,** of the Kingdom of Ireland, died near Reading, Berkshire, on 24 January 1766. [SM.28.55]

**Farnham, the Earl of,** married Mrs Upton a widow, in Ireland in December 1771. [SM.33.670]

**FARQUHARSON, ALEXANDER,** Captain of the Aberdeenshire Fencibles, died in Ireland on 31 December 1799. [SM.61.909]

**FARQUHARSON, .....,** daughter of Mrs Farquharson of the 25th Regiment, was born in Ennis on 15 November 1824. [SM.94.766]

**FARRELL, ANDREW,** aged 107, died in Dalgenny, Ireland, on 19 December 1765. [SM.27.671]

**FARRIER, Lieutenant General,** died in Castle Iver, King's County, in 1805. [SM.67.967]

**FERGIE, WILLIAM,** died in County Down in December 1780. 'his gross weight was six hundred weight'. [SM.43.54]

**FERGUSON, Sir ANDREW,** baronet, was killed in an accident near Londonderry, 18 July 1808. [SM.70.638]

**FERGUSON, CHARLES,** a merchant in Cork, died there on 2 January 1794. [SM.56.62]

**FERGUSON, Dr ROBERT,** aged 88, died in Cork, 1810. [SM.72.880]

**FERNE, Reverend GEORGE,** aged 100, died in Dublin on 14 October 1769. [SM.31.559]

**Ferrard, Viscountess MARGARET,** Baroness of Oriel, aged 87, died at Collan, County Louth, on 29 January 1824. [SM.93.256]

**FIFFE, JAMES,** in Dublin, married Jean Steven, only daughter of Mr Steven an architect, in Edinburgh in 1794. [SM.56.235]

**FINCH, GEORGE,** brother of the Earl of Aylesford, died in Dublin on 16 September 1823. [SM.92.512]

**Fingal, Earl of,** of the Kingdom of Ireland, died 1739. [SM.I.93]

**Fingal, Countess Dowager of,** of Ireland, died 1749. [SM.11.407]

**Fingal, the Earl of**, an Irish peer, married Miss Woolacott, only child and heir of William Woolacott of Woolhampton, Berkshire, in London on 20 March 1755. [SM.17.159]

**Fingal, the Earl of,** died in Dublin on 21 August 1793. [SM.55.466]

**FINLEY, Captain WILLIAM,** died near Donard, County Wicklow, on 21 October 1763. 'He was descended from the ancient family of the Finley of Kirkcudbright in Scotland'. [SM.25.583]

**FITZGERALD, Lady AUGUSTA,** youngest daughter of the Duke of Leinster, died in Leinster House, Dublin, on 7 March 1790. [SM.52.154]

**FITZGERALD, Lord AUGUSTUS,** son of the Duke of Leinster, died in Dublin in May 1771. [SM.33.390]

**FITZGERALD, Lady CAROLINE,** daughter of the Earl of Kildare, died in Dublin on 13 April 1754. [SM.16.204]

**FITZGERALD, Lord EDWARD,** married Pamela, the natural daughter of M. Egalite the ci-devant Duc d'Orleans, in Tournay, Flanders, in 1792. [SM.55.49]

**FITZGERALD, Reverend GERALD,** aged 80, DD, Rector of Ardstragh, died in Moyle House, County Tyrone, on 10 March 1819. [SM.83.386]

**FITZGERALD, Lady GERALDINA,** third daughter of the Duke of Leinster, died in Leinster House, Dublin, on 23 March 1790. [SM.52.155]

**FITZGERALD, JAMES,** Duke of Leinster, Marquis and Earl of Kildare, died in Dublin on 19 November 1773. [SM.35.616]

**FITZGIBBON, Miss,** daughter of the Lord Chancellor of Ireland, died in 1790. [SM.53.49]

**FITZMAURICE, THOMAS,** married Lady Mary O'Brian, daughter of the Earl of Inchiquin, on 21 December 1777. [SM.39.678]

**FITZPATRICK, JOHN,** Earl of Upper Ossory, an Irish peer, MP, died at Amphill Park, Bedfordshire, on 23 September 1758. [SM.20.500]

**FITZGERALD, ROBERT,** eighteenth Earl of Kildare, died in Cartown, County Kildare, on 20 January 1744. [SM.6.98]

**FITZGERALD, Lord ROBERT STEPHEN,** fourth brother of the Duke of Leinster, married Miss Fielding, daughter of Mrs Sophia Fielding of St James' Place, and niece to the Earl of Winchelsea, on 22 June 1792. [SM.53.360]

**FITZGERALD, WILLIAM ROBERT,** Duke of Leinster, born March 1748, Member of Parliament for Dublin pre 1776, member of the House of Peers, married Emilia Oliva St George in November 1778, died in Carlton, County Kildare, on 20 October 1804. [SM.66.887]

**FITZGIBBON, PHILIP,** a mathematician and a compiler of an Irish dictionary, died in Kilkenny in 1792. 'He has willed his dictionary and many other curious manuscripts to the Reverend Mr O'Donnell'. [SM.53.206]

**FITZMAURICE, THOMAS,** Earl of Kerry, died at Lixnaw, Kerry, 1741. [SM.4.142]

**FITZMAURICE, WILLIAM,** Earl of Kerry, died at Lixnaw on 5 April 1747. [SM.9.198]

**FITZPATRICK, HUGH,** an eminent bookseller, died in Dublin in 1818. [SM.82.589]

**FITZPATRICK, Miss,** sister of the Earl of Offory, married the Earl of Shelburne on 7 July 1779. [SM.41.399]

**FITZWILLIAM, JOHN,** Colonel of the 2nd Regiment of Foot, died in Ireland on 17 July 1757. [SM.19.438]

**FITZWILLIAM, Lord Viscount RICHARD,** a Privy Councillor in Ireland, died at Mount Merrion on 25 May 1776. [SM.38.279]

**FITZWILLIAM, Earl,** married Lady Ponsonby, at Bishop's Court near Dublin on 21 July 1823. [SM.92.383]

**FLANAGAN, PATRICK,** aged 104, a lime burner, died in Waterford in 1789. [SM.51.623]

**FLANAGAN, ......,** three sons of Patrick Flanagan in Mabbot Street, Dublin, were born on 25 December 1804. [SM.67.73]

**FLEMING, DANIEL,** from Cork, nephew to General Fleming in Swedish service, married Clementina Forbes from Dunbar, in London on 11 May 1755. [SM.17.268]

**FLEMING, JAMES,** aged 18, married Mrs Katherine Bibby, a widow, aged 78, in Dublin in August 1753. [SM.15.422]

**FLEMING, Mrs MARY,** aged 115, died in Mitchell's town, County Cork, on 6 April 1770. [SM.32.229]

**FLEMING, THOMAS,** Alderman and former Lord Mayor of Dublin, died there on 24 July 1809. [SM.71.640]

**FLEMING, WILLIAM,** Lord Slane, died in Ireland 1747. [SM.9.98]

**FLETCHER, Dr THOMAS,** Bishop of Kildare, died in Dublin on 8 March 1761. [SM.23.166]

**FLETCHER, Judge,** aged 75, Judge of the Court of Common Pleas, died in County Dublin on 6 June 1823. [SM.92.128]

**FLOOD, Sir FREDERICK,** late MP for County Wexford, died in Dublin on 31 January 1824. [SM.93.383]

**FLOOD, HENRY,** aged 57, died in Farmly on 2 December 1791. [SM.53.621]

**FLOWER, WILLIAM,** Lord Baron of Castledurrow, died 29 April 1746. [SM.8.250]

**FLOWER, WILLIAM,** born 25 June 1744, succeeded to the peerage 27 June 1752, Lord Viscount Ashbrook, Baron of Castle Durrow in Ireland, died in September 1780. 'He married a Miss Rudge by whom he has left issue – two sons and four daughters'. [SM.42.505]

**FLOYDE, Lieutenant General,** married Lady Denny, widow of the late Sir Barry Denny baronet, in Dublin on 11 July 1805. [SM.67.726]

**FOLLIOTT, Lieutenant General JOHN,** Governor of Ross Castle, Lieutenant Governor of Kinsale, a Major General on the Irish Establishment, and Colonel of the 13th Regiment of Foot, died in Dublin on 26 February 1762. [SM.24.167]

**FOORD, Captain,** Providore of the Royal Hospital near Dublin, died 1740. [SM.2.95]

**FOOT, LUNDY,** aged 70, an eminent tobacconist and alderman of Dublin, died there on 8 January 1805. [SM.67.79]

**FORAN, Captain WILLIAM,** of George Street, Dublin, died in 1811. [SM.73.720]

**FORBES, ANGOULEME,** youngest son of the Earl of Granard, died on 14 April 1810. [SM.72.478]

**FORBES, GEORGE,** Earl of Granard, Privy Councillor, and senior Admiral of the Navy, died in Dublin on 29 June 1765. He had succeeded his father Arthur Forbes on 24 August 1737, he married the eldest daughter of William, the first Viscount Mountjoy and relict of Phineas Preston of Ardallagh, County Meath, she died on 4 October 1758, the couple had two sons Major General George, Lord Forbes, now Earl of Granard, Colonel of the 29th Regiment of Foot, and John, Admiral of the Blue. His lordship was MP in the British Parliament for Queensborough in 1724, and for Ayr in 1741, he was appointed minister plenipotentiary to the Czarina. [SM.27.336]

**FORBES, GEORGE,** Earl of Granard, a Privy Councillor in Ireland, baronet of Nova Scotia, died in Castle Forbes, County Longford, on 15 April 1780. [SM.42.223]

**FORBES, HENRY,** brother of the Earl of Granard, married Miss E. Pearson, sister of John Preston the Member of Parliament for Navan, in Bellinter, County Meath, 1794. [SM.57.67]

**FORBES, Lord,** eldest son of the Earl of Granard, married Lady Selina Rawdon, second daughter of the Earl of Moira, in Ireland in June 1779. [SM.41.341]

**FORBES, .....,** daughter of Lady Forbes, was born in Cork on 16 June 1813. [SM.75.556]

**FORD, JOHN,** aged 100, married Miss Egan of Mullingar, aged 19, in Dublin on 2 November 1753. [SM.15.581]

**FORD, JOHN RAWDON,** Captain of the 82$^{nd}$ Regiment, died at Ballynahinch in 1811. [SM.73.400]

**FORD, Mrs,** wife of ..... Ford in County Down, died in Dublin 1808. She was eldest daughter of the late William Brownlow, and mother of 20 children. [SM.70.557]

**FORRESTER, Dr NICHOLAS,** Bishop of Raphoe, died 1743. [SM.5.295]

**FORTESCUE, Rear Admiral Sir CHARLES,** aged 70, Ulster King of Arms, died in Collenswood near Dublin in 1820. [SM.85.488]

**FORTESCUE, GERALD,** Ulster King of Arms and chief Herald of Ireland, died in Dublin in 1787. [SM.49.570]

**FORTESCUE, MATHEW,** of Stephenstoun, Ireland, married Catherine Eglantine Blair, eldest daughter of William Blair of Blair, at Blair, Ayrshire, on 7 December 1811. [SM.73.958]

**FORTESCUE, THOMAS JAMES,** Member of Parliament for Louth, and nephew of Lord Clermont, died in Dublin in 1795. 'An apothecary's boy sold his servant laudanum instead of tincture of rhubarb, which the unfortunate gentleman swallowed'. [SM.57.545]

**FOSTER, Dr JOHN,** aged 95, formerly a Fellow of Trinity College, Dublin, and Rector of Omagh, died in Ireland in 1788. [SM.50.570]

**FOSTER, THOMAS HENRY,** only son of John Foster the Chancellor of the Exchequer of Ireland, married Miss Skeffington, only child of Chichester Skeffington, and niece of the Earl of Masserene and the Earl of Roden, in Annandale, Ireland, on 20 November 1810. [SM.72.957]

**FOSTER, Reverend Dr,** Bishop of Clogher, died in Ireland in 1797. [SM.59.931]

**FOULKE, FRANCIS,** from Dublin a student of medicine at the University of Edinburgh, president of the Natural History Society and of the Royal Medical Society of Edinburgh, was killed in a duel on Leith beach on 22 December 1789. [SM.51.622]

**FRANKS, ANTHONY,** married Louisa Percy, only daughter of E. H. Percy of Dublin, there on 8 April 1826. 'Mr Franks walked for two successive Sundays on St Stephen's Green, in quest of a fair partner to solace his solitary hours'. [SM.97.766]

**FRASER, JAMES,** Lieutenant Colonel of the Fraser Fencibles, died at Cove Villa, Kinsale, on 1 September 1805. [SM.67.727]

**FRASER, STEPHEN,** aged 102, a bachelor, born in Ireland, died in Chatham on 30 July 1778. [SM.40.390]

**FRASER, .....,** aged over 118, an invalid, died at the Royal Hospital at Kilmainham near Dublin on 27 September 1768. [SM.30.503]

**FRENCH, ARTHUR,** MP, died in County Roscommon in 1821. [SM.87.296]

**FRENCH, CHARLES,** eldest son of Lord French, married Maria, eldest daughter of John Browne of Moyne, at Salthill near Galway on 29 September 1809. [SM.71.877]

**FRENCH, JOHN,** late Lieutenant Colonel of the 71$^{st}$ Regiment, died in Drogheda on 15 January 1812. [SM.74.157]

**FRENCH, Mrs MARY,** aged 104, died at Milton, County Kildare, on 15 December 1757. [SM.19.670]

**FRENCH, Baroness ROSE,** of Castle French, died in Dublin on 8 December 1805. Her title devolved to her eldest son Sir Thomas, now Lord French. [SM.67.968]

**FRENCH, THOMAS,** aged 105, died in Dublin, 21 December 1807. [SM.70.238]

**FRIEND, JOHN,** aged 26, died in Dublin on 18 May 1772. [SM.34.333]

**FULLER, Miss,** an authoress, died near Cork in 1790. [SM.52.363]

**FURZER, HENRY REDDISH,** Lieutenant Colonel of the Royal Marines, died in Kinsale on 9 January 1820. [SM.85.191]

**GAGE, HENRY,** aged 47, Viscount Gage of Castle Island, Baron of Castlebar in Ireland, and a Major General, died in London, 22 February 1808. His son, Henry Hall aged 17, succeeds him. [SM.70.317]

**GALAHER, TERENCE,** aged 116, died in Dungannon on 21 February 1776. [SM.38.163]

**GALE, JOSEPH,** aged 129, died in County Mayo on 16 January 1769. 'He had been tenant to Lord Westport and his ancestors about 100 years'. [SM.31.110]

**Galway, ......,** son of Lord Galway, born 1741. [SM.4.94]

**Galway, Viscount,** Baron of Killard in Ireland, died at Salthill on 3 March 1774 when bound for Bristol. [SM.36.166]

**Galway, ......,** daughter of Viscountess Galway, was born on 22 November 1784. [SM.46.606]

**GARDINER, LUKE,** married Miss Montgomery, daughter of William Montgomery and sister of Lady Townshend, in Dublin in July 1773. [SM.35.390]

**GARVEY, NICHOLAS,** of Tully, County Mayo, aged 107, died on 23 November 1816. [SM.79.79]

**GAUCHAN, THOMAS,** aged 112, died near Crossmonna, County Mayo, on 16 August 1814. [SM.76.578]

**GAVEN, MICHAEL,** aged 19, married Mrs Anne Dardis, aged 91, of Francis Street, Dublin, in September 1766. [SM.28.503]

**GEMINIANA, Signior FRANCISCO,** aged 96, a musician, died in Dublin on 17 September 1762. [SM.24.507]

**GEMMILL, ROBERT,** aged 64, a merchant in Belfast, died there on 30 May 1808, 'in consequence of a fall from a vessel in the quay'. [SM.70.479]

**GENTLEMAN, ......,** a Captain of Ottway's Regiment of Foot, died in Dublin on 21 December 1746. [SM.9.49]

**GEORGES, HAMILTON,** Member of Parliament for County Meath, died in Dublin in 1802. [SM.64.616]

**GERNON, Mr,** aged 125, died in County Louth on 28 June 1780. [SM.42.389]

**GIBSON, JAMES,** Major of the Dunbarton Fencibles, eldest son of James Gibson a surgeon in Edinburgh, died in Antrim in 1800. [SM.62.652]

**GILBERT, CLAUDIUS,** DD, Professor of Divinity at the University of Dublin, died 1743. [SM.5.428]

**GILBURNE, THOMAS,** aged 104, died in Cork during 1787. 'he served in Queen Anne's Wars, under the Duke of Marlborough, and fought at the battle of Dettingen in 1743. [SM.49.623]

**GILES, KATHARINE,** aged 122, died in Glanwhorry near Connor in the county of Belfast on 13 December 1757. [SM.20.51]

**GILLESPIE, ROLLO,** formerly a Captain of the 17th Regiment of Foot, died at Coomber in Ireland, 1810. [SM.72.719]

**GILLESPIE, WILLIAM,** born 1710 in Ireland, a soldier in the Enniskillen Dragoons, fought in Germany 1743-1744 under Lord Stair, and at the Battle of Prestonpans in 1745, a Chelsea Pensioner, died in Ruthwell, Dumfries-shire, on 15 June 1818. [SM.82.294]

**GILMOUR, PATRICK,** from Londonderry, married Christie Hamilton Dalrymple, eldest daughter of Charles Dalrymple, Gill's Cottage, County Londonderry, in Ayr on 18 October 1819. [SM.84.487]

**GILSHENAN, RICHARD,** aged 120, died in Donell, Ireland, in August 1771. [SM.33.502]

**GISBORNE, Major General,** married Miss Boyd, daughter of Charles Boyd, in Dublin on 12 February 1771. [SM.33.109]

**Glandore, JOHN, Earl of,** Viscount Crosbie, Baron Brandon, a Privy Councillor of Ireland, aged 63, husband of Diana Sackville, died at Ardfert Abbey on 23 October 1815. [SM.77.958]

**GLASGOW, Mrs,** relict of Reverend John Glasgow late of Coleraine, died in Cookstown on 10October 1817 of typhus. [SM.17.399]

**GLEDSTONES, ......,** son of Major N. Gledstones of the 68th Regiment, was born at Castlehill on 11 December 1818. [SM.83.94]

**GLENNY, JAMES,** a merchant, died in Newry in 1802. [SM.64.528]

**GLENTWORTH, Reverend** Baron, Bishop of Limerick, married the relict of General Crump in Kilmutry church near Limerick on 14 October 1792. [SM.53.570]

**GOFF, ......,** possibly the largest man in Ireland .... his coffin measured six feet eight inches in length and one yard and half a quarter wide, and was carried by twelve strong men, died in Dublin in July 1782. [SM.44.447]

**GORDON, Lieutenant Colonel JOHN,** of the 81st Regiment of Foot, died in Kinsale on 31 October 1778. [SM.40.628]

**GORDON, Captain JOSEPH,** aged between 90 and 100, died at the Royal Hospital in Dublin on 23 February 1752. 'He raised and maintained a company

at his own expense at the Siege of Derry'.
[SM.14.101]

**GORDON, PATRICK,** a merchant in Dublin, married
Harriet Maria Cowley, second daughter of the late
Lieutenant Colonel Cowley of Mount Pleasant,
County Dublin, on 29 July 1813. [SM.75.717]

**GORDON, WILLIAM,** of Sheep Bridge in Ireland,
married Mary Elisabeth Gillespie, daughter of Dr
Thomas Gillespie a physician, in Edinburgh on 14
February 1787. [SM.49.101]

**GORDON, .....,** daughter of Lieutenant Colonel
Gordon of the 5th [Prince Leopold's] Regiment of
Dragoon Guards, was born in Dublin on 24 November
1822. [SM.90.126]

**GORE, ARTHUR,** the Earl of Arran, died in Saunders
Court, County Wexford, on 1 April 1773. 'leaving issue
Arthur Saunders Gore, Lord Sudley, who succeeds
him, Richard and Paul Gore, and Lady Anne Dally'.
[SM.35.278]

**GORE, JOHN,** Baron Annsley, Lord Chief Justice of
King's Bench in Ireland, died in Dublin on 3 April
1784. [SM.46.223]

**GORE, Lieutenant General,** Governor of Kinsale, died
1739. [SM.I.375]

**Gormanstown, Lord,** died at his seat near Drogheda
on 2 November 1757. [SM.19.614]

**GOSFORD, Lord Viscount ARCHIBALD,** born 1718,
created Baron Gosford of Markethill in 1776, and
Viscount Gosford in 1785, died at Gosford Castle,
County Armagh, on 4 September 1790. [SM.52.465]

**GOUGH, JOHN,** aged 129, died in Castletown, County Waterford, in October 1771. [SM.33.614]

**GOWER, ROGER,** aged 111, an eminent attorney, died in Dublin on 26 June 1779. [SM.41.342]

**GRAHAM, Major DAVID,** of the 50th Regiment of Foot, married Honoria Stokes, daughter of Oliver Stokes in County Kerry, at Sackville House, County Kerry, on 5 July 1824. [SM.94.254]

**GRAHAM, HECTOR,** Registrar of the Court of Common Pleas, and father in law of Lord Chief Justice Norbury, died in Dublin on 29 September 1806. [SM.67.808]

**GRAHAM, JAMES,** of Richardby House, Cumberland, a Captain of the 2nd North British Dragoons [the Scots Greys], married Elizabeth Jane Saurin, second daughter of the Lord Bishop of Dromore, in Dromore Cathedral in 1821. [SM.88.293]

**GRAHAM, Mrs MARGARET,** spouse of Dr John McRobert, assistant surgeon of the 2nd Battalion of the 92nd Regiment, died in Listubu on 24 April 1808. [SM.70.399]

**GRAHAM, Major,** an old officer, died in Dublin, 1739. [SM.I.623]

**GRAHAM, Captain,** of the Dunbarton Fencibles, married Miss MacArtney, daughter of Reverend Dr MacArtney, in Antrim in 1802. [SM.63.180]

**GRAHAM, ......,** son of Brigadier General Graham, was born in Cork on 5 January 1809. [SM.71.78]

**GRAHAM, ......,** son of Major General Graham, was born in Cork on 10 January 1813. [SM.75.157]

**Granard, the Earl of,** died in Ireland on 22 October 1769. His title and estate went to his son Lord Forbes a Lieutenant Colonel in the Guards. [SM.31.559]

**Granard, ......,** son of the Earl of Granard, was born in Dublin on 30June 1801. [SM.63.516]

**GRANDISON, .....,** son of Viscount Grandison, was born in Dublin on 12 July 1750. [SM.12.349]

**GRANDISON, ......,** son of Viscount Grandison, was born in Dublin on 13 December 1751. [SM.13.597]

**GRANDISON, the Countess of,** died in Dublin on 14 January 1768. [SM.30.110]

**GRANT, JAMES,** late Captain of the 85th Regiment, married Miss D. Flood, second daughter of Captain Flood of the 52nd Regiment, in Dublin in June 1807. [SM.69.559]

**GRANT, ......,** son of Charles Grant of Ballygoran, was born in Newry in May 1773. [SM.35.277]

**GRANT, Major,** of the 41st Regiment, married Miss Odell, daughter of the late John Odell of Odell Lodge, in Kilmurry in 1799. [SM.61.652]

**Grattan,** Dowager, aged 70, sister to Henry Grattan, died in Dublin on 23 October 1813. [SM.75.960]

**GRAY, Reverend FRANCIS,** aged 74, for over 40 years pastor of the Presbyterian congregation of Boveagh, died in Camnish, Dungiven, on 26 July 1817. [SM.80.99]

**GRAY, J.,** aged 55, a shoemaker, died in Louth on 6 December 1823. [SM.93.128]

**GRAY, Dr WILLIAM,** a physician, died in Dublin on 3 April 1805. [SM.67.327]

**GREEN, WILLIAM,** aged 84, a clerk in the Council Office in Dublin, died there on 15 July 1794. [SM.56.443]

**GREENFIELD, Reverend ANDREW,** died in Moira, Ireland, on 11 May 1788. [SM.50.259]

**Greenock, .....,** daughter of Lady Greenock, was born in Dublin on 22 April 1823. [SM.91.174]

**GRESDALL, THOMAS,** aged 106, formerly surveyor of Ringsend, Ireland, died there on 22 August 1757. [SM.19.438]

**GREY, Major,** of the 80$^{th}$ Regiment, married Miss Vignoles, in Portarlington on 27 December 1808. [SM.71.77]

**GRIERSON, BOULTER,** HM Printer in Ireland, died in Bray on 22 June 1771. [SM.33.333]

**GRIERSON, GEORGE,** aged 74, the King's printer in Ireland, died in Dublin on 27 October 1753. [SM.15.581]

**GRIFFITH, Mrs,** relict of Richard Griffith, died in Milliescent, Ireland, on 5 January 1793. [SM.55.50]

**GROSVENOR, HENRY,** aged 115, surveyor of the coast at Blackwater, died in Inch, County Wexford, on 16 September 1780. 'He was of French extraction, very sparing in his diet, and used much exercise; no one preserved more what the French call the youth of old age, being an agreeable cheerful companion at the age of 100 when he married his last wife'. [SM.42.505]

**GUNNING, Miss,** aged 98, aunt to the late Duchess of Hamilton and Argyle, died in Dublin in 1797. [SM.59.636]

**HAIRE, HAMILTON,** of Glassdrummond, married Anne Chittick, second daughter of M Chittick, Enniskillen, County Fermanagh, in St Mary's Church, Dublin, on 1 March 1824. [SM.93.511]

**HALEY, MAURICE,** father of three sons born in Cork on 16 August 1770. [SM.32.457]

**HALL, MARY,** aged 101, 'remarkable for having twenty-four fingers, thumbs and toes', died in St Katherine's parish, Dublin, 1741. [SM.3.279]

**HALL, Dr,** Lord Bishop of Dromore, died in Dublin on 21 November 1811. [SM.74.79]

**HALLAM, JAMES,** aged 103, died in Maryborough on 2 February 1776. [SM.38.109]

**HALLYBURTON, Major DOUGLAS GORDON,** brother of the Earl of Aboyne, married Louisa, only child of Sir Edward Leslie of Tarbert, County Kerry, in Dublin on 16 July 1807. [SM.69.636]

**HAMILTON, GAWIN,** of Killileagh Castle, County Down, aged 78, died in London on 9 April 1805. His son Archibald Hamilton Rowan inherited. [SM.67.327]

**HAMILTON, Reverend GEORGE,** late of Armagh, died on 8 November 1817 in Carrickfergus of typhus. [SM.80.501]

**HAMILTON, GUSTAVUS,** late Major of Tyrawley's Dragoons, died in Dublin on 30 September 1754. [SM.16.500]

**HAMILTON, GUSTAVUS,** eldest son of Lord Viscount Boyle, married Miss Somerville, only daughter of Sir Quayle Somerville deceased, in Dublin on 31 March 1773. [SM.35.165]

**HAMILTON, Dame HELEN,** aged 80, widow of Sir Walter Hamilton of Westport, died there on 13 December 1770. [SM.32.684]

**HAMILTON, HENRY,** aged 104, died in Drumboy in 1820. [SM.85.488]

**HAMILTON, Reverend HUGH,** DD, FRS, MRLA, Lord Bishop of Ossory, formerly a Fellow of Trinity College, Dublin, and Professor of Natural Philosophy, died at the Palace, Kilkenny, on 13 December 1805. [SM.67.157]

**HAMILTON, J.F.,** of Westport, married Georgina Vereker, second daughter of Lord Gort, in Limerick on 2 August 1817. [SM.80.97]

**HAMILTON, Colonel J.P.,** Professor of German at Dublin University, died in Dublin on 27 September 1787. He was formerly in the service of the King of Prussia and fought at the battle of Hochkirchen under his kinsman Marshal Keith. [SM.49.467]

**HAMILTON, JAMES,** Viscount Strabane in Ireland, died in London on 11 January 1744. [SM.6.50]

**HAMILTON, JAMES,** Earl of Clanbrasil, an Irish peer, died at St Stephen's Green, Dublin, on 18 March 1758. He was succeeded by his only son James, Lord Viscount Limerick, Chief Remembrancer of the Exchequer in Ireland. [SM.20.161]

**HAMILTON, JAMES,** Earl of Clanbrasil, died in Dublin in 1798. [SM.60.214]

**HAMILTON, JAMES,** aged 91, died in Strabane on 22 March 1806. He married Eleanor, sister to the Earl of Castlestewart, in 1750. [SM.67.319]

**HAMILTON, JAMES,** Captain of the 3$^{rd}$ Garrison Battalion, eldest son of the late James Hamilton of Stevenston, Lanarkshire, died in Waterford in May 1807. [SM.25.479]

**HAMILTON, JOHN,** Member of Parliament for Strabane, married Miss Hamilton, daughter of Lord Viscount Boyne, in Dublin in November 1770. [SM.32.630]

**HAMILTON, Sir JOHN CHARLES,** of Dunnemnan, Ireland, died in London on 13 December 1818. [SM.83.96]

**HAMILTON, OTHO,** aged 82, Lieutenant Governor of Placentia in Newfoundland, formerly Major of the 40$^{th}$ Regiment, died in Waterford on 7 February 1770. [SM.32.111]

**HAMILTON, RICHARD,** Lord Viscount Boyne, died in Ireland on 31 August 1789. He was succeeded in title and estate by his eldest son Gustavus. 'This family is descended from the family of Abercorn in Scotland'. [SM.51.412]

**HAMILTON, ......**Rector of Dunleer, and brother of the late Earl of Abercorn, died on 22 May 1746. [SM.8.250]

**HAMILTON, Mrs,** sister of Lord Castlestewart, and wife of J. Hamilton of Strabane, died in Dublin during 1789. [SM.51.259]

**HAMILTON, Mrs,** aged 78, relict of Colonel Otho Hamilton of Olivestob, died on 11 March 1819. [SM.83.386]

**HANGER, GABRIEL,** Lord Coleraine, died in Maidenhead on 24 January 1773. [SM.35.54]

**HANGER, Miss,** sister of Lord Coleraine, married Arthur Van Stittart, on 2 August 1773. [SM.35.445]

**HANNA, MARTHA,** aged 126, died near Cullybackey on 11 March 1808. She was born near Dungannon. Her height was 4 feet 7 inches. [SM.70.318]

**HARDING, PETER,** aged 113, a farmer, died near Cork on 4 August 1755. [SM.17.414]

**HARE, PRUDENCE,** aged 119, died in Lisnagregan near Randalstown on 15 May 1821. [SM.88.93]

**HARKNESS, WILLIAM,** of Dublin, an eminent merchant and a Director of the Bank of Ireland, died on 12 October 1817. [SM.80.399]

**HARLEY, JOHN,** a merchant in Dublin, married Bridget Bell of Glasgow, in 1807. [SM.69.637]

**Hartland, Lord Baron MAURICE,** died at Strokestown House, County Roscommon, on 4 January 1819. He married Catherine Moore, daughter of Stephen, Lord Mount Cashel, in 1765, and they had three sons – Major General Thomas Mahon, Lieutenant Colonel of the 9th Dragoons; Major General Stephen Mahon, Lieutenant Colonel of the 7th Dragoon Guards; and Reverend Maurice Mahon, prebentary of St Patrick's Cathedral. [SM.83.192]

**HARTLEY, JAMES,** Deputy Governor of the Bank of Ireland, died on 12 February 1811. [SM.73.238]

**HAWKE, Lieutenant Colonel,** of the 62nd Regiment of Foot, second son of Admiral Hawke, died in Dublin on 2 October 1773. [SM.35.559]

**HAWKINS, Reverend Dr JAMES,** Bishop of Raphoe, died in Ireland on 29 June 1807. [SM.69.639]

**HAY, ALEXANDER,** second mate of the Norfolk Indiaman, second son of Alexander Hay of Whittingham near Berwick, died at Kinsale on 6 December 1758. [SM.20.660]

**HEATH, Rear Admiral,** of Fahan, County Londonderry, died 12 June 1815. [SM.77.559]

**HEATLY, Mrs,** relict of William Heatly, first cousin to the Duke of Argyll, and daughter of William Montgomery of Rosemount, died in Dublin in 1805. [SM.67.79]

**HENLEY, JAMES,** aged 24, married .... Benson, a widow aged 105, in Dublin on 7 April 1757. [SM19.219]

**HERLINY, DANIEL,** aged 107, a laborer, died in Cork in 1787. [SM.49.623]

**HEWITT, JAMES,** aged 80, Lord Viscount Lifford, Lord High Chancellor of Ireland, died in Dublin on 29 May 1789. [SM.51.258]

**HEWITT, Justice,** of the King's Bench in Ireland, died on 1 April 1794. [SM.56.236]

**HIBBUTTS, ISAAC,** aged 100, a laborer, died in County Galway in 1790. 'In the last 30 years he has had 7 wives and by each of them children'. [SM.52.517]

**HICKMAN, HERBERT,** Lord Viscount Windsor, Baron Mountjoy, of the Kingdom of Ireland, died at Bath on 25 January 1758. [SM.20.52]

**HILL, CHARLOTTE,** eldest daughter of the Marchioness of Downshire, Baroness Sandys, died in Frankfort on 30 May 1821. [SM.88.496]

**HILL, TREVOR,** Lord Viscount Hillsborough, died at Hillsborough, Ireland, 5 May 1742. [SM.4.242]

**HILL, WILLS,** aged 75, Marquis of Downshire, Earl and Viscount Hillsborough and Baron Kilwarlin in Ireland, died at his seat of Hillsborough on 7 October 1793. [SM.55.517]

**HILL,.....,** daughter of Lord Viscount Hillsborough, was born in Dublin in September 1750. [SM.10.398]

**HILLMAN, JOHN,** aged 115, of Leitrim, County Londonderry, died on 9 March 1821. [SM.87.495]

**Hillsborough, Lord Viscount,** married Lady Margaret Fitzgerald, sister to the Earl of Kildare, in Dublin on 3 March 1748. [SM.10.153]

**HINDS, ELIZABETH,** aged 106, died in Dublin in 1785. [SM.47.206]

**HOADLY, Dr JOHN,** Archbishop of Armagh and Primate and Metropolitan of All Ireland, died at Rathfarnham on 19 July 1746. [SM.8.349]

**HOARE, CHARLES,** aged 119, died in Wexford on 19 February 1765. [SM.27.111]

**HOBBS, THOMAS,** Captain of the 92nd Highlanders, married Margaret Hacket, third daughter of Simpson Hacket, Rivers Town, Tipperary, at Cork 1819. [SM.83.583]

**HOGG, Major FOUNTAIN,** of the 26th Regiment, married Miss Carleton, daughter of J. Carleton, in Dublin in 1808. [SM.70.316]

**HOG, WILLIAM FORBES,** a merchant, died in Dublin in February 1795. [SM.57.275]

**HOLLAND, JOHN,** aged 105, and his wife aged 85, died in Moyard near Rathfryland, 1739. [SM.2.47]

**HOLMES, RENE,** of Kilmuklan, aged 130, died in King's County, on 25 January 1753. [SM.15.54]

**HOLMES, Reverend WILLIAM,** aged 85, minister of the Associate Presbyterian Congregation of Ballyeaston, died in Islandmagee on 30 November 1823. [SM.93.128]

**HOMAN, Mrs,** aged 85, grand-niece to the late Lord Chancellor Hyde, and second cousin to Queen Anne, died at the house of Charles Lennon in County West Meath in 1787. [SM.49.361]

**HOME, WILLIAM,** barrack master of Newry, late of the 86th [Royal County Down] Regiment, married Hopewell Glenny, daughter of Isaac William Glenny, on19 November 1824. [SM.94.767]

**HOOD, THOMAS PELHAM,** of Springmount, County Antrim, married Miss Kennedy, daughter of John Kennedy of Underwood, there on 4 February 1824. [SM.93.383]

**HOOD, Mrs,** sr., of Springmount, County Antrim, died there on 29 January 1825. [SM.95.383]

**HOPE, ....,** son of Lady Hope, was born in Dublin on 4 October 1812. [SM.74.804]

**HOPPER, ANTHONY,** aged 115, died in Cork on 11 September 1779. 'who fought under King William at the Battle of the Boyne, he continued in the service during the wars in Ireland, after which he served under the Duke of Marlborough in Germany'. [SM.41.511]

**HORE, ......,** son of Mrs Hore of Harperstown, was born in Wicklow on 12 January 1813. [SM.23.157]

**HOTHAM, Dr,** Bishop of Clogher, died in Bath in 1795. [SM.57.749]

**HOWARD, CHARLES,** only son of Charles Howard, next heir to the Duke of Norfolk, married Miss Coppinger, 'a very great heiress', in Dublin on 29 July 1767. [SM.29.446]

**HOWARD, Lady LOUISA,** died in Abeville near Dublin in 1781. [SM.43.390]

**HOWARD, ......,** Lord Viscount Wicklow, died in Dublin on 26 July 1789. He was son of Dr Robert Howard, Bishop of Elphin. He was succeeded in his titles and estate by his eldest son Robert Howard. [SM.51.361]

**HOWE, GEORGE AUGUSTUS,** Lord Viscount Howe, an Irish peer, Colonel of the 55th Regiment of Foot, a Brigadier on the American Establishment, was killed in action near Ticonderoga on 6 July 1758. [SM.20.442]

**Howth, ......,** son of Lord Howth, was born in Ireland on 4 October 1752. [SM.14.510]

**Howth, ......,** son of the Earl of Howth, was born in Dublin on 20 January 1807. [SM.69.77]

**HOY, Miss,** daughter of Mr Hoy a stationer in Dublin, married the Earl of Shrewsbury in Bordeaux on 7 October 1792. [SM.53.569]

**HUBERT, MATTHEW,** aged 121, died in Birr on 28 November 1764. [SM.26.632]

**HUME, ANDREW,** a merchant, died in Sligo on 13 January 1809. [SM.71.159]

**HUSSEY, JAMES,** brother of Lord Beaulieu, and nephew to the last Baron of Galtrim, died at his seat in Baldoyle, Ireland, on 5 April 1787. His considerable fortune devolved to his younger brother Richard Hussey. [SM.49.206]

**HUSSEY, .....,** daughter of Edward Hussey, Duke of Manchester, was born in Dublin on 27 August 1749. [SM.11.406]

**HUSSEY,.........,** daughter of Thomas Hussey of Galtrim in Ireland, and grand-daughter of Lord Orford, married Reverend William Wodehouse, youngest son of Lord Wodehouse, at Wolterton, Norfolk, on 11 February 1807. [SM.69.157]

**HUTCHESON, FRANCIS,** Professor of Moral Philosophy at the University of Glasgow, died in Dublin on 8 August 1746. [SM.8.398]

**HUTCHINSON, CHRISTIAN HELY,** Baroness Donoghmore of Knocklofty, died in Palmerston, Ireland, on 24 June 1788. She is succeeded by her eldest son Richard Hely Hutchinson, Commissioner of the Revenue, now Baron Donoghmore. [SM.50.311]

**HUTCHINSON, Sir FRANCIS,** aged 80, died in Dublin on 18 December 1807. [SM.70.79]

**HUTCHINSON, JOHN HELY,** Secretary of State for Ireland, a Privy Councillor in Ireland, Member of Parliament for Cork, and Provost of Trinity College, Dublin, died in London on 5 September 1794, aged 79. His spouse Baroness Donughmore died in 1788. [SM.56.655]

**HUTCHINSON, A. A. HELY,** youngest son of A. A. Hely Hutchinson, brother of Lord Donoughmore, died in North Great George Street, Dublin, on 14 January 1821. [SM.87.191]

**HUTCHINSON, Reverend L. HELY,** youngest brother of the Earl of Donoughmore, died in Dublin on 28 November 1822. [SM.91.128]

**HYNES, THADIE,** aged 105, died in Cork in January 1767. [SM.29.103]

**Ikerrin, Lord Viscount,** married Anne Wynne, eldest daughter of Owen Wynne of Haslewood, County Sligo, and niece of the Earl of Enniskillen, in Dublin on 1 September 1811. [SM.73.716]

**Inchiquin, WILLIAM, Earl of,** Knight of the Bath, married Miss Moore, daughter of Stephen Moore, at Moorepark near Kilworth, Ireland, on 12 October 1761. [SM.23.558]

**Inchiquin, the Earl of,** Lord Lieutenant and custos rotolorum of County Cork, died at his seat near Cork on 19 July 1777. He was succeeded by his nephew Murrough O'Brian. [SM.39.390]

**INGLIS, GEORGE,** assistant surgeon of the 57th Regiment, died in Macroom on 19 August 1823. [SM.92.511]

INGLIS, Mrs MARGARET, wife of James Gordon, late Superintendant of Water in Edinburgh, and daughter of the late William Inglis a surgeon in Edinburgh, died in Londonderry on 27 March 1807. [SM.69.318]

INNES, CHARLES, died in Dromartine near Newry in May 1804. [SM.66.479]

INNES, Colonel JAMES, aged 73, died at Coleraine on 15 July 1762. [SM.24.451]

IRVING, GEORGE, Captain of the Royal Irish Artillery, married Miss Hamilton of Milnburn on 1 April 1798. [SM.60.291]

IRVING, SOPHIA, daughter of George D'Arcy Irving of Castle Irving, County Fermanagh, married Arthur Hinn Trevor, eldest son of Lord Viscount Dungannon, in Leghorn on 10 September 1821. [SM.88.495]

IRWIN, ALEXANDER, a Lieutenant General and Colonel of a Regiment of Foot, died in Ireland, 1752. [SM.14.318]

Iveagh, MARGARET, the Dowager Viscountess, aged 70, died in Kilcath, County Tipperary, on 19 July 1744. [SM.6.346]

IVIE, HENRY, of Mount Alto in Ireland, married Helen Nicolson, daughter of the deceased Sir William Nicolson of Glenbervie, in Montrose on 11 February 1781. [SM.43.110]

JACKSON, WILLIAM, Colonel of the North Mayo Militia, married Jane Louisa Blair, third daughter of William Blair of Blair, Ayrshire, in Louth Church, Ireland, on 9 October 1815. [SM.77.874]

JACKSON, Mrs, widow of the Lord Bishop of Kildare, died in Bath in 1805. [SM.67.886]

**JACKSON, ......,** son of Captain H. G. Jackson, was born at Island Bridge near Dublin on 17 February 1820. [SM.85.291]

**JAMES, JAMES FRENCH,** died at his house near Cork on 27 August 1793. [SM.55.414]

**JAMES, THOMAS,** aged 100, died in Carnew, County Wicklow, in 1790. He was the father of Alderman James of Dublin. [SM.53.50]

**JAMESON, ALEXANDER,** a Lieutenant of O'Ffarrel's Regiment of Foot, died of a shot received in a duel with William Sprowle an attorney, in Dublin 28 September 1754. 'He sailed round the world with Commander Anson'. [SM.16.500]

**JAMESON, J.,** a Baron of the Exchequer in Ireland, died in Dublin in 1823. [SM.92.512]

**JENKINS, CALEB,** an Alderman of Dublin, died there on 11 March 1792. [SM.53.205]

**JEPHSON, ROBERT,** a gentleman and an author, died in Dublin Castle in 1803. [SM.65.364]

**JERVIS, HENRY MEREDYTH JERVIS WHITE,** eldest son of Sir John Jervis of Ballyellis, County Wexford, married Marion Campbell, third daughter of the late William Campbell of Fairfield, Ayrshire, in Edinburgh on 16 December 1818. [SM.83.95]

**JERVIS, Sir J.,** baronet, married Isabella, relict of the late John Jervis Ruckley, and cousin german to Lord St Vincent, in Moynoe Hall, County Clare, on 18 February 1811. [SM.73.318]

**JOCELYN, Lady ANN,** aged 24, only sister of the Earl of Jocelyn, died in Dublin, on 21 October 1822. [SM.90.751]

**JOCELYN, J. BLIGH,** a Lieutenant in the Royal Navy, second son of the Earl of Roden, died in Dundalk on 10 July 1812. [SM.74.647]

**JOCELYN, .....,** son of Lord Viscount Jocelyn, was born in Ireland in July 1768. [SM.30.389]

**JOHNSON, Dr ROBERT,** Bishop of Cloyne, died at Cloyne, in Ireland, on 20 January 1767. [SM.29.56]

**JOHNSON, .....,** a poor woman age 123, died in Pound Street, Belfast, 1807. 'Her brother, who is still alive, is 100 years, and his wife is the same age'. [SM.69.876]

**JOHNSTON, ARTHUR,** MD, of Carrickbreda, County Armagh, and Tremont, County Down, married Sarah Maria Whellier, third daughter of Thomas Whellier late of Exeter, in Edinburgh on 22 April 1826. [SM.97.767]

**JOHNSTON, Captain GEORGE,** aged 87, died at Monkstown near Dublin on 7 June 1770. He was son of Sir Patrick Johnston, Lord Provost of Edinburgh in the beginning of Queen Anne's reign, and father of General James Johnston now Lieutenant Governor of Minorca, also of Lady Napier and Mrs Johnston of Hilton. [SM.32.343]

**JOHNSTON, JAMES BROWN,** surgeon and Lieutenant of the 2nd Battalion Rothesay and Caithness Fencibles, married Eliza Green, youngest daughter of Michael Green of Middleton, County Cork, on 5 July 1798. [SM.60.507]

**JOINT, Lieutenant,** of the Roscommon Militia, married Miss Fraser, daughter of ...... of the Fraser Fencibles, in Kinsale in 1809. [SM.71.638]

**JONES, JOHN,** aged 102, died in Cloonterk, County Mayo, on 12 September 1773. [SM.35.501]

**JONES, Mrs SARAH,** aged 102, died in Dublin in 1789. [SM.52.50]

**JONES, VALENTINE,** aged over 80, of Belfast, died in Portpatrick, 2 November 1808. [SM.70.879]

**JUDGE, ROBERT,** aged 95, of Cooksburgh near Kilbeggan, married Miss Ann Nugent aged 15, in Ireland 1769. 'He served in King William's wars and received a ball in his nose.' [SM.31.110]

**KAVANAGH, THOMAS,** of Borris, County Kilkenny, married Lady Harriet Trench, second daughter of the Earl of Clancarty, at Garpally the seat of the Earl of Clancarty , on 28 February 1825. [SM.95.310]

**KEARNEY, JAMES,** aged 115, died in Ireland on 19 March 1770. 'He lately had a daughter married, aged 15'. [SM.32.167]

**KEARNEY, Right Reverend Dr JOHN,** Bishop of Ossory, aged 72, Fellow of Dublin College in 1764, Professor of Oratory in 1781, Provost in 1799, died in the Episcopal Palace, Kilkenny, on 22 May 1813. [SM.75.479]

**KEATING, JAMES,** aged 103, a soldier, died in the Royal Hospital, Dublin, on 28 April 1773. [SM.35.278]

**KEATING, WILLIAM POWER,** Earl of Clancarty, Viscount Dunlo, Lord and Baron Kirkconnel, died in Dublin on 25 April 1805. [SM.67.565]

**KELLETT, WILLIAM AUGUSTUS,** died in Cork on 5 November 1822. [SM.89.752]

**KELLY, Captain DENNIS,** who in 1722 was committed to the Tower but was acquitted, died in Connaught, 1740. [SM.2.387]

**KELLY, Mrs MARGARET,** died in Dawson Street, Dublin, in December 1797, a few hours later Mrs French, widow of Colonel French, died in St Andrew's Street, Dublin. 'The history of these two ladies is somewhat remarkable. Two officers of the $22^{nd}$ Regiment stationed in Minorca in 1756 married two nuns of St Clair from the convent of Citadella in that island; these two nuns were the ladies whose death we record..... Mrs French was present at the taking of Havannah in 1762'. [SM.59.931]

**KELLY, PETER,** MD, surgeon in the Royal Navy, occulist to the Cork Eye Dispensary, late physician of the Fever Hospital, Newmarket, County Cork, died in Cork of consumption in 1823. [SM.92.640]

**KELLY, Mr,** aged 105, died in County Meath in 1796. [SM.58.218]

**KELLY, Mrs,** widow of Dr Kelly, died in Limerick on 7 January 1821 'in consequence of her head-dress taking fire from a candle which she held in her hand'. [SM.87.294]

**KEMP, RONALD,** a merchant in Belfast, died in Comrie, Ross-shire, on 6 October 1803. [SM.65.739]

**KENDALL, OLIVER S.,** aged 92, a mariner, died in Warrenpoint on 8 September 1823. 'fought under Admiral Rodney in his engagement with De Grasse, and also circumnavigated the globe three times'. [SM.92.512]

**KENNEDY, JAMES,** aged 84, a historical painter, married Miss Mary Alder, aged 76, at Stewartstown church, County Tyrone, on 12 July 1823. [SM.92.383]

**KENNEDY, Captain JOHN,** of Springhall, District Paymaster in Dublin, died there on 17 June 1806. [SM.67.566]

**KENNEDY, Mrs,** aged 87, sister of Sir Archibald Edmonstone of Duntreath baronet, died in Coleraine on 28 March 1802. [SM.64.276]

**KEON, Miss ANNE,** died at St Stephen's Green, Dublin, on 26 August 1793. [SM.55.414]

**KER, Colonel,** died in Dublin on 4 February 1745. [SM.7.98]

**KERR, Captain MARK,** of the 9th Dragoons, son of the deceased Robert Kerr of Newfield, died in Carlow on 20 August 1791. [SM.53.467]

**KERR, ROBERT,** surgeon of the 1st Regiment of Light Dragoons, died in Clonmell on 19 July 1803. [SM.65.587]

**KER, WILLIAM,** Captain of Boscawen's Regiment of Foot, son of the late Lord Charles Ker, died in County Wicklow on 18 June 1754. [SM.16.308]

**Kerry, the Earl of,** married Mrs Daly, sister of the Countess of Louth and of the Viscountess of Kingsland, on 24 March 1768. [SM.30.165]

**KILBEE, ELLEN,** second daughter of James Kilbee in Belfast, married Robert Stuart a merchant in Glasgow, in Sandyford, Glasgow, on 14 September 1815. [SM.77.873]

**Kildare,......,** son and heir of the Earl of Kildare, was born in Dublin on 15 January 1748. [SM.10.50]

**Kildare, ......,** son of the Earl of Kildare, was born at Kildare House on 15 February 1752. [SM.14.156]

**Kildare, ......,** daughter of the Earl of Kildare, was born in Dublin on 6 December 1753. [SM.15.627]

**Kildare, ....,** son of the Earl of Kildare, was born at his seat of Cartown, County Kildare, on 30 June 1756. [SM.18.367]

**Kildare, the Countess-Dowager,** grandmother to the present Earl and sister to the late Earl of Coningsby, died in London on 10 April 1758. [SM.20.220]

**Kildare, ........,** daughter of the Earl of Kildare, was born in Dublin on 9 October 1762. [SM.24.567]

**Kildare, ........,** son of the Earl of Kildare, was born in London on 15 October 1763. [SM.25.583]

**Kildare, the Dowager Lady,** mother of the Countess of Hillsborough, died in Ireland on 10 February 1780. [SM.42.110]

**Killala, the Bishop of,** married Miss Obins, in Bath on 30 July 1805/ [SM.67.726]

**Killeen, Lord,** only son of the Earl of Fingal, married Louisa Corbally, only daughter of Elias Corbally, in Corbalton, County Meath, on 11 December 1817. [SM.81.94]

**KILLIGREW, GEORGE AUGUSTUS,** aged 40, Major of a regiment of carabineers on the Irish establishment, died on 9 August 1757. [SM.19.438]

**Kilmain, Lord,** died in Dublin on 23 June 1794. [SM.56.375]

**Kilmore, .....,** daughter of the Bishop of Kilmore, was born in Dublin in 1793. [SM.55.360]

**KING, Sir PATRICK,** Justice of the Peace for County Dublin, and Commissary General of Musters, died in Leixslip in 1790. [SM.52.207]

**KING, Sir ROBERT,** Lord Kingsborough, an Irish peer, died at his seat at Boyle, County Roscommon, on 22 May 1755. His estate and title went to his brother Edward. [SM.17.268]

**KING, Mr T.,** clerk to his uncle Edward King, died in Tralee in 1803. [SM.65.739]

**KING, Colonel,** aged 88, brother of Edward the Earl of Kingston, and uncle of Viscount Lorton, a former Governor of County Sligo and Colonel of the Sligo Militia, died in Rockingham, County Roscommon, on 23 February 1821. [SM.87.399]

**Kingsborough, Lord,** son of the Earl of Kinghorn, married Miss Fitzgerald, daughter of Colonel Fitzgerald, in Ireland in December 1769. [SM.31.671]

**Kingsland, Lord Viscount,** died in Quanbury, County Galway, on 11 March 1774. [SM.36.166]

**Kingsland, Lord Viscount,** of the Kingdom of Ireland, died in Port L'Orient, France, in 1797. [SM.59.360]

**Kingston, the Earl of,** died at his seat in County Roscommon on 20 December 1797. [SM.59.931]

**Kingston, ROBERT, the Earl of,** died in Cork in 1799. [SM.61.284]

**Kinsale, .....,** son of Lord Kinsale, was born in October 1768. [SM.28.558]

**Kinsale, Lady,** died in Kinsale 'at an advanced age' on 15 December 1819. [SM.85.95]

**KIRKPATRICK, ALEXANDER,** aged 116, formerly Colonel of an Irish regiment of foot under the Duke of Marlborough, died in Longford in 1782. [SM.45.392]

**KIRKPATRICK, ALEXANDER,** an Alderman of Dublin, died in Coolmine on 10 July 1818. [SM.82.200]

**KIRWAN, PATRICK,** of Creggs, County Galway, died in Dublin on 22 November 1755, as a result of a duel with Edward Brereton, Deputy Serjeant at Arms, in Lucas's Coffee House. [SM.17.564]

**KIRWAN, RICHARD,** of Cregg, County Galway, Fellow of the Royal Society, President of the Royal Irish Academy, President of the Dublin Literary Society, and a member of every literary body in Europe, died in Dublin on 1 June 1812. [SM.74.646]

**KIRWAN, Reverend WALTER BLAKE,** Dean of Killala, died in Dublin on 27 October 1805. [SM.67.886]

**Knapton, Lord,** married Miss Brooke, daughter of Sir Arthur Brooke, in Ireland in October 1769. [SM.31.558]

**KNOX, Reverend CHARLES,** son of Lord Viscount Northland, and brother of the Bishop of Derry, also Member of Parliament for the University of Dublin, married Mrs James Fletcher, daughter of Robert Bent, Member of Parliament for Aylesbury, in December 1804. [SM.67.72]

**KNOX, Cornet JAMES,** died aged 88, 'he was at the raising of the Royal Irish Dragoons, served in nineteen campaigns in King William's and Queen Anne's wars'. [SM.15.628]

**KNOX, THOMAS,** aged five, third son of Reverend E. Knox, and grandson of Lord Viscount Northland, died from vitriol poisoning, at Dungannon Park in 1814. [SM.76.880]

**KNOX, THOMAS,** Member of Parliament for County Tyrone, eldest son of Thomas Knox, and grandson of Lord Viscount Northland, married Mary Juliana, eldest daughter of the Lord Primate of All Ireland, and grand-daughter of John, late Earl of Bute, in Armagh on 28 February 1815. [SM.77.318]

**KNOX, WILLIAM,** second son of the Bishop of Derry, married Miss S. Ferguson, second daughter of the late Sir A. Ferguson, in the Cathedral Church, Londonderry, on 24July 1811. [SM.73.558]

**LACY, DAVID,** aged 113, died in Limerick on 14 December 1759. [SM.21.663]

**LACY, Count,** aged 84, born in Munster, Ireland, moved to France in 1691, an officer of the French Army under the Duke of Berwick until the Peace of Ryswick, thereafter commanded a regiment of foot soldiers in the service of the Emperor, finally Czar Peter I commissioned him as a Colonel, died 30 April 1751. [SM.13.309]

**LAMBERT, GUSTAVUS,** of Beaupark, married Ann Butler Stevenson, second daughter of Sir John Stevenson, in Dublin in 1810. [SM.73.76]

**LAMBERT, RICHARD,** nephew to the late Earl of Cavan, died near Paris in June 1768. [SM.30.335]

**Lambert, Lord, Earl of Cavan,** died in Dublin on 29 September 1772. He was succeeded in titles and dignities by his cousin german Major General Richard Mambert of the Foot Guards. [SM.34.518]

**LAMONT, JAMES,** master of the Lucy of Charlestown, lately stranded on the coast of Scotland, died in Larne on 25 August 1803. [SM.65.588]

**Lanesborough, HUMPHREY, Earl of,** died in Dublin on 11 April 1768. He was succeeded by his only son Lord Viscount Newton. [SM.30.223]

**Lanesborough, ......,** daughter of the Earl of, was born in Dublin on 8 September 1769. [SM.31.502]

**Lanesborough, ....,** son and heir of Lord Viscount Lanesborough of Ireland, was born in London on 11 July 1771. [SM.33.390]

**Lanesborough, the Earl of,** married Miss Latouche, in Dublin in January 1781. [SM.43.54]

**LANESBURY, Lady Dowager,** aged 83, died in Dublin on 24 December 1759. [SM.21.663]

**LANGLANDS, MATTHEW,** a merchant in Limerick, married Janet Watson, second daughter of William Watson jr, a merchant, in Campbeltown on 6 August 1823. [SM.92.383]

**LANGRISHE, Sir HERCULES,** baronet, died at St Stephen's Green, Dublin, on 31 January 1811. [SM.73.159]

**LANGSTON, JOHN,** aged 82, from Nottingham, a trooper in King William's army and that of Queen Anne, he fought at the battles of Hochster, Malplaquet and Blenheim, died in Dublin on 12 January 1754. [SM.16.50]

**LANIGAN, Reverend Dr JAMES,** aged 74, titular Bishop of Ossory, died in Kilkenny on 20 January 1812. [SM.74.238]

**LATOUCHE, DAVID,** aged 88, a Privy Councillor and an MP in Ireland for 40 years, died at St Catherine's, Ireland, on 1 August 1817. [SM.80.99]

**LATOUCHE, PETER DIGGES,** died 'in an apoplectic fit' in Dublin on 5 February 1820. [SM.85.295]

**LATOUCHE, WILLIAM DIGGES,** died in Dublin on 16 November 1803. [SM.65.816]

**LATOUCHE, ......,** twin sons of Lady Emily Latouche, were born in Harristown, County Kilkenny, on 16 September 1814. [SM.76.876]

**LAUGHLIN, ISABELLA,** aged 118, died near Rathfryland, County Down, on 20 April 1752. She had 110 children, grand-children, and great-grand-children. Her grandfather, father, and husband were brogue-makers. She was buried in a leather coffin.' [SM.14.213]

**LAW, EDWARD,** Member of Parliament, eldest son of Lord Ellenborough, married Lady Octavia Stewart, youngest daughter of the Earl of Londonderry, in London on 11 December 1813. [SM.76.77]

**LAW, Miss M.,** youngest daughter of William Law, married James Law of the East India Company Civil Service, in Dunmore near Londonderry on 13 November 1808. [SM.70.957]

**LAW, MICHAEL,** eldest son of Robert Law a banker, married Jane Hannah Hamilton, second daughter of Hans Hamilton MP for Dublin, at Castleknock Church in Dublin on 13 September 1819. [SM.84.358]

**LAWLER, MARGARET,** aged 135, died in Kilkevan, County Wexford, 1739. [SM.I.584]

**LAWRENCE, PETER,** a Rear Admiral on half pay, died at his seat in County Galway on 23 November 1758. [SM.20.660]

**LAZENBY, GEORGE,** of Parliament Street, Dublin, married Miss Griglietti of the Theatre Royal on 7 September 1817. [SM.80.294]

**LEARMONTH, JOHN,** from Edinburgh, married Margaret Cleghorn second daughter of James Cleghorn MD, the state physician, at St Mary's church, Dublin, on 24 February 1824. [SM.93.511]

**LECKEY, OLIVER,** of Strabane, married Miss Baird of Castlefin in March 1802. [SM.64.372]

**LEE, JOHN,** Colonel of a regiment of foot, died on 5 August 1750 in Ireland. [SM.12.398]

**LEE, .....,** Major of Murray's Regiment, died in Ireland, 1752. [SM.14.318]

**LEES, Sir JOHN,** baronet, died in Dublin on 3 September 1811, 'at a very advanced age', his was succeeded in title by his son Reverend Harcourt Lees. [SM.73.718]

**LEES, .....,** son and heir of John Lees secretary to the Lord Lieutenant of Ireland, was born in Dublin Castle on 29 November 1776. [SM.38.622]

**LEES, Mrs,** wife of Sir John Lees baronet, died at Black Rock near Dublin in 1805. [SM.67.887]

**LEESON, ROBERT,** of Clermont, County Wicklow, youngest son of the late Earl of Miltown, married Phillippa Juliana Rose, youngest daughter of the late

Reverend J. Rose, Prebendary of Worcester, at Turvey House on 28 October 1810. [SM.72.877]

**LEFANU, ALICIA,** wife of Joseph Lefanu, and sister of Richard Brinsley Sheridan, died at her son's house, Royal Hibernian School, Dublin, on 4 September 1817. [SM.80.196]

**LEIFER, ALEXANDER,** formerly accountant of the Stirling Bank, later manager of the Provincial Bank of Ireland in Waterford, died there on 1 March 1826. [SM.97.511]

**Leinster, ......,** son of the Duke of Leinster, was born at Leinster House, Dublin, in December 1767. [SM.29.669]

**Leinster, ......,** daughter of the Duke of Leinster, was born in Dublin in January 1770. [SM.32.111]

**Leinster, .....,** son of the Duke of Leinster, was born in Ireland on 14 April 1773. [SM.35.223]

**Leinster, ......,** daughter of the Duke of Leinster, was born in Ireland on 28 August 1779. [SM.41.455]

**Leinster, .......** daughter of the Duke of Leinster, was born in Carton, Ireland, on 8 September 1787. [SM.49.516]

**Leinster, .....,** daughter of the Duke of Leinster, was born in Leinster House, Dublin, on 27 February 1789. [SM.51.153]

**Leinster, .......** son of the Duke of Leinster, was born in Carton, Ireland, on 21 August 1791. [SM.53.466]

**Leinster, ......,** son of the Duke of Leinster, was born in Carlton, Ireland, on 4 January 1793. [SM.55.49]

**Leinster, .....,** son of the Duke of Leinster, was born in 1796. [SM.58.360]

**Leinster, ......,** son of the Duke of Leinster, was born in Rutland Square, Dublin, on 30 March 1819. [SM.83.478]

**LEITH, ......,** son of Sir George Leith baronet, was born in Armagh on 30 October 1806. [SM.67.886]

**LEITH, Colonel,** of the Aberdeenshire Fencibles, married Lady Augusta Forbes, sister of the Earl of Granard, in Londonderry on 13 February 1798. [SM.60.213]

**LENOX, ......,** a daughter of Lady Charlotte Lenox, was born in Dublin on 22 August 1792. [SM.53.413]

**LENOX, ......,** a son of Lady Charlotte Lenox, was born at the Vice-Regal Lodge, Phoenix Park, Dublin, on 30 September 1793. [SM.55.568]

**LESLIE, Dr JAMES,** Bishop of Limerick, Ardsert, and Aghadoc, died in Dublin on 24 December 1770. [SM.32.684]

**LETT, Mrs ELIZABETH,** aged 104, died in Seafield, Ireland, on 8 January 1819. She had 56 children and grand-children, her youngest child, Charles Lett, was delivered when she was 59. [SM.83.192]

**LEVINGE, Sir RICHARD,** baronet, married Elizabeth Anne Parkins, sister of Lord Rancliffe, at Castle Forbes, the seat of the Earl of Granard in Ireland, on 3 December 1810. [SM.73.76]

**LEWIS, Captain HENRY CHARLES,** district paymaster, died from a fall from his horse in Waterford on 15 July 1804. [SM.66.656]

**LIFFORD,........,** daughter of Lord Lifford, Lord High Chancellor of Ireland, was born in 1769. [SM.31.166]

**LINCOLN, Dr,** titular Archbishop of Dublin, died there on 21 June 1763. [SM.25.360]

**LINDSAY, Colonel,** late of the 22nd Regiment of Foot, died in Dungannon on 31 May 1804. [SM.66.566]

**LINDSAY, ......,** son of Lieutenant Colonel Martin Lindsay of Halbeath, of the 78th Regiment, was born in Tullamore on 25 August 1818. [SM.82.294]

**LINDSAY, ........,** daughter of Thomas Spencer Lindsay, was born in Hollymount House, County Mayo, on 14 February 1819. [SM.83.284]

**LINDSAY, ......,** daughter of Lieutenant Colonel Lindsay of the 78th Highlanders, was born at Royal Barracks in Dublin on 13 May 1821. [SM.87.589]

**LINDSAY, Dr.,** Bishop of Kildare, died in Glasnevin on 6 January 1825. He was brother of the Earl of Balcarras and brother-in-law to the Earl of Hardwick. [SM.95.256]

**LINEGAR, Dr .....,** titular Archbishop of Dublin, died there in June 1757. [SM.19.383]

**LISMORE, Miss,** daughter of Lord Lismore of Ireland, died in Exeter on 14 June 1793. [SM.55.308]

**Lismore, Lord,** died in Shanbelly, County Tipperary, in 1797. [SM.59.636]

**Lismore, ....** daughter of Lord Viscount Lismore, was born in Henrietta Street, Dublin, on 12 December 1811. [SM.73.957]

**LITTLE, Miss RACHEL,** 'who was six feet four inches high', died at Old Castle, County Meath, on 10 February 1756. [SM.18.108]

**LITTLEHALES, Sir EDWARD BAKER,** baronet, married Lady Elizabeth FitzGerald, daughter of the Duke of Leinster, at Loftus Hill near Dublin on 15 July 1805. [SM.67.725]

**LIVINGSTONE, Reverend SAMUEL,** minister of the Presbyterian congregation of Clare, County Armagh, died in 1802. [SM.64.447]

**LLOYD, JOHN,** Captain of Fowke's Regiment of Foot, died at Waterford on 22 May 1755. [SM.17.268]

**LOFTUS, DUDLEY,** of Lillyon, County Meath, married Jean Gore, youngest daughter of the Earl of Arran by his first wife, the sister of the Earl of Annesley, in Dublin on 6 July 1793. [SM.55.359]

**LOFTUS, Lord Viscount NICHOLAS,** an Irish peer, died in County Wexford on 25 January 1757. [SM.19.54]

**LOFTUS, NICHOLAS,** Lord Viscount Loftus of Ely, County Wexford, died in Dublin on 31 December 1763. 'He is succeeded by his eldest son Nicholas'. [SM.26.55]

**LOFTUS, NICHOLAS,** Earl of Ely, died in Dublin on 31 October 1766. [SM.28.615]

**LOFTUS, NICHOLAS,** Earl of Ely, Viscount Loftus of Ely, and Baron Loftus of Loftus Hall, died in Dublin on 12 November 1769. [SM.31.615]

**Londonderry, the Countess of,** died on 18 May 1772. 'greatly lamented by the poor'. [SM.34.277]

**Londonderry, ROBERT, the Marquis of,** died at Mountstewart on 6 April 1821. [SM.87.496]

**Longford, Lord Viscount,** married Miss Rowley, daughter of Hercules Longford Rowley, and sister to the Countess of Bective, and at the same time and place Miss Packenham, his lordship's sister, married William Sherlock, in Ireland in June 1768. [SM.30.334]

**Longford, .....,** son of the Countess of Longford, was born in Rutland Square, Dublin, on 26 September 1822. [SM.89.630]

**LORKAN, JOHN,** aged 112, died at Meelick in July 1755. [SM.17.460]

**LOVE, LOVELACE,** died in Brookhill on 9 July 1784. 'He was noted for his extraordinary bulk, weighing upwards of 40 stone. His coffin measured seven feet in length, four feet across and three and a half feet deep. His death was occasioned by his immense corpulency.' [SM.46.391]

**Lowth, ....,**son of Lord Lowth, was born at Lowth Hall, Ireland, in September 1757. [SM.19.495]

**Lowth, the Lady Dowager,** died at Lowth Hall, County Lowth, on 12 February 1767. [SM.29.110]

**Lowth, ......,** a daughter of the Earl of Lowth, was born in Dublin on 30 July 1767. [SM.29.446]

**Louth, .......,** son of the Earl of Louth, was born on 29 October 1810. [SM.72.957]

**Lucan, the Earl of,** of the Kingdom of Ireland, died in London on 29 March 1799. 'He is succeeded by his son Lord Bingham'. [SM.61.284]

**LUCAS, Dr.**, married Miss Kelly aged 18, in Ireland on 7 October 1768. [SM.30.559]

**LUCAS, Dr CHARLES,** died in Dublin on 5 November 1771. [SM.33.614]

**LUCY, Dr,** titular bishop of Limerick, died there on 4 August 1759. [SM.21.444]

**LUTTON, Mrs,** aged 90, died in County Kildare in 1764. [SM.26.463]

**LUTTRELL, SIMON,** Earl of Carhampton, of Castlehave, Viscount and Baron Inham of Luttrellstown, father of the Duchess of Cumberland. He was created a Baron in 1768, a Viscount in 1781, and an Earl ion 1785. He was succeeded by his eldest son Henry Lawes Luttrell, a Major General, Lieutenant Colonel of the 1st Regiment of Horse, and a Privy Councillor. [SM.49.51]

**LYNCH, DENNIS,** aged 101, died in Kilcullen, Ireland, in 1787. [SM.49.361]

**LYON, JOHN,** aged 116, died at Bandon on 22 July 1761. 'Born in Londonderry, he served at the siege of that fortress, the breach of the Boyne, the battle of Aoghrim, and all the wars of Ireland, under King William III.' [SM.23.446]

**MCALLISTER, Reverend HUGH,** Presbyterian minister of Loughbrickland, died on 10 February 1824. [SM.94.512]

**MACAVOY, SUSANNAH,** a beggar, aged 120, died in Dublin on 14 October 1751. [SM.13.502]

**MACBRIDE, FANNY,** died in Rossgull, County Donegal, in 1787. 'After a night's dancing she fell into a kind of trance or lethargy, in which she continued for ten days; on the eleventh she awakened as it were from a long sleep, yawned two or three times, rubbed her hands, and then expired'. [SM.49.311]

**MCCALL, SAMUEL,** late of Glasgow, died in Limerick on 2 May 1805. [SM.67.566]

**MCCALL, .....,** son of James McCall, Fitzwilliam Street, Dublin, was born on 28 March 1818. [SM.81.294]

**MACCARTHY, DANIEL BULL,** aged 112, died in the barony of Iveragh, County Kerry, in February 1752. 'He had been married to five wives, the fifth when he was 84 and she 14, by whom he had about 20 children.' [SM.14.101]

**MACCARTHY, Mrs,** aged 103, widow of Captain MacCarthy of Cove Street, died in Cork in 1787.[SM.49.570]

**MCCARTHY, Mrs CATHERINE,** aged 102, widow of Michael McCarthy formerly a revenue officer in Dublin, died in Tracton on 22 February 1820. [SM.85.389]

**MACARTNEY, Sir JOHN,** aged 63, formerly Deputy Remembrancer of the Court of the Exchequer in Ireland, died in Ramsey on 29 May 1812. He was succeeded in title by his eldest son Reverend William Macartney. [SM.74.645]

**MACARTNEY, Count,** of Ireland, aged 104, died in Turin on 4 October 1766. [SM.28.558]

**MACCARTNEY, General,** aged 97, born in Ireland, for many years in Hungarian service, died in February 1771. [SM.33.110]

**MACARTNEY, Miss,** daughter of the late Dr MacArtney of Antrim, married John Cheyne, MD, in Leith on 3 November 1804. [SM.66.971]

**MCCASKILL, .....,** son of Colonel McCaskill, was born in Belfast in 1808. [SM.70.878]

**MCCAUSLAND, JOHN,** 'for many years Member of Parliament for County Donegal', died in Douglas, Isle of Man, in 1804. [SM.67.75]

**MCCAY, Miss,** daughter of Reverend McCay of Philipsburg, Dublin, married the Earl of Belvidere on 10 November 1803. [SM.65.814]

**MCCLURE, ALEXANDER,** aged 24, late of Newry, died in Barbados in 1802. [SM.64.447]

**MCCUBBIN, ROBERT,** of the Army Accounts Office in Dublin, only son of Reverend William McCubbin minister of Douglas, Lanarkshire, died in Dublin on 16 April 1805. [SM.67.565]

**MCCULLOCH, Mrs ELIZABETH,** wife of James Dalzell a surgeon of the 32nd Regiment, and daughter of the late Henry McCulloch of Torhousekie, died in Dublin in 1803. [SM.65.364]

**MCCULLOCH, Captain,** of the Ross and Cromarty Regiment, married Miss McVeagh, daughter of the late Joseph McVeagh of Drewstoun, in Lurgan on 5 January 1802. [SM.64.180]

**MCCULLOUGH, WILLIAM,** aged 70, married Miss Rice of Westpark, at Skiliganaban bear Ballynure, in 1810. [SM.72.478]

**MCDANIEL, NANNY,** aged 106, died in St Patrick's Hospital, Dublin, in 1796. 'She was twice married, both times to a soldier. Her first husband was killed at Fontenoy, and her second at the battle of Prestonpans, where she likewise lost a son'. [SM.58.289]

**MACDERMOT, CHARLES,** of Shruse, aged 98, alias the Prince of Coolavin, died in County Sligo on 13 February 1758. [SM.20.110]

**MCDONALD, JAMES,** aged 117, seven feet six inches high, formerly a soldier from 1685 to 1716, lately a day-laborer, died near Cork on 15 August 1760. [SM.22.447]

**MACDONALD, PATRICK,** aged 108, died in Baltimore, Ireland, on 16 August 1784. [SM.46.448]

**MACDONNELL, ALEXANDER,** Earl of Antrim, a Privy Councillor, Governor of County Antrim, died in Dublin on 14 October 1775. 'he was succeeded in titles and estate by his only son William Randall MacDonnell, Lord Viscount Dunluce, Member of Parliament for County Antrim. [SM.37.582]

**MACDONNELL, MARY,** aged 118 years, born in Skye, Inverness-shire, settled in County Down in 1688, died at Magheratempenny near Ballynohinch, County Down, on 16 May 1785. [SM.47.311]

**MACDONNELL, RANDALL,** Marquis of Antrim, Privy Councillor, Governor of County Antrim, died in Antrim House, Merion Square, Dublin, on 28 August 1791. He was born on 4 November 1749, married Letitia Trevor, daughter of Harvey, Viscount Mountmorres, on 3 July 1774. [SM.53.414]

**MACDONNEL,........,** daughter of Lieutenant Colonel MacDonnel the Assistant Adjutant General, was born in Dublin in December 1806. [SM.69.77]

**MACDONOUGH, JOAN,** aged 138, died near Ennis on 11 April 1768. [SM.30.223]

**MCDOWALL, Reverend BENJAMIN,** DD, senior minister of the Scots Church, Mary's Abbey, died in Dublin in 1824. [SM.94.640]

**MCDOWALL, LAWRENCE,** Lieutenant Colonel of the Renfrewshire Regiment of Militia, died in Athlone on 5 August 1815. [SM.77.875]

**MCFARLANE, ROBERT,** aged 127, a farmer, died in Donnoghmore, Donegal, in December 1804. [SM.67.76]

**MACFARLANE, ROBERT,** son of the late Andrew MacFarlane of Auchrossan, died at Cove of Cork on 2 February 1826. [SM.97.384]

**MCFINDLAY, CHARLES,** aged 143, died in Tipperary in June 1773. 'he was a captain in the reign of King Charles I, and went with Oliver Cromwell into Ireland, soon after which he retired from the army'. [SM.35.335]

**MCGIVERN, EDWARD,** aged 114, died in Lisburn on 17 July 1818. 'his wife is still living and healthy, in Lisburn, aged 109'. [SM.82.200]

**MCGLAUGHLIN, MICHAEL,** aged 105, a shoemaker, died in Athlone on 22 May 1775. 'he had five wives the last of whom he has left with a child not above a year and a half old.' [SM.37.286]

**MCGRATH, CORNELIUS,** the late Irish giant, [seven feet eight inches tall], born in County Tipperary in 1736, died in College Green, Dublin, on 20 May 1760. [SM.22.272]

**MACGRATH, ROBERT,** of Kilbaaron, County Clare, aged about 115, died in January 1752. 'He was a student in the Temple at the restoration of King Charles II, was married, and had a daughter in 1664, and another in 1717'. [SM.14.53]

**MACGREGOR, .....,** daughter of Lieutenant Colonel MacGregor, was born in Dublin on 7 February 1825. [SM.95.382]

**MACGUIRE, Colonel,** late of the Queen of Hungary's service, married Lady Cathcart on 18 May 1745. [SM.7.249]

**MCHARG, JAMES,** a Lieutenant of the 99th Regiment, died in Dublin on 19 December 1794. [SM.56.802]

**MCILROTH, Mrs,** aged 93, relict of Colonel McIlroth, died in Belfast on 10 November 1821. [SM.88.620]

**MCINTYRE, DUNCAN,** late of Leith, a merchant in Sligo, died there on 21 May 1812. [SM.74.645]

**MACKAY, JAMES,** eldest son of Alexander Mackay publisher of the *Belfast Newsletter*, died on 6 December 1806 aged 19. [SM.69.78]

**MCKECHIE, JANE,** aged 107, died in Clonmell on 9 February 1799. [SM.61.144]

**MCKEE, Mrs MARY,** aged 110, died in Celbridge, County Kildare, in October 1780. [SM.42.563]

**MACKENNA, Right Reverend Dr MATTHEW,** Titular Bishop of Cloyne, died at Cove near Cork in 1791. [SM.53.311]

**MCKENZIE, ALEXANDER,** of Saintfield, aged 120, died in Belfast on 28 March 1754. 'He left a widow who is but 4 years younger than himself.' [SM.16.155]

**MACKENZIE, RONALD,** formerly a Captain of the 68th Regiment, died in Killough, Ireland, on 17 September 1798. [SM.60.719]

**MACKENZIE, Lieutenant Colonel,** of Wrighton, married Miss Hay, daughter of Major David Hay of the Angus-shire Fencibles, in Dublin in 1806. [SM.67.806]

**MACLEAN, JOHN,** aged 109, died in Orange County, New York, in August 1770. 'He was a drummer in King William's army in Ireland'. [SM.32.630]

**MCLEAN, JOHN,** quarter-master of the 92nd Regiment, died at Tuam, 22 July 1808. [SM.70.639]

**MACLEOD, ......,** daughter of Major General MacLeod of the 78th Regiment, was born in Athlone on 7 September 1819. [SM.84.387]

**MACLONGHLID, JAMES,** aged 136, died in Dublin on 16 April 1758. 'he served as a sergeant in King William's army at the battle of the Boyne.' [SM.20.220]

**MACMAHON, HONOR,** aged 110, died in Granaham, near Limerick, on 25 November 1769. [SM.31.671]

**MCNALLY, LEONARD,** aged 68, of the Irish Bar, died in Dublin on 15 February 1820. [SM.85.295]

**MACNAMARA, M.,** a Lieutenant General in the French Army, died at Rochfort on 18 October 1756. [SM.18.524]

**MCNAMARA, TIMOTHY,** aged 112 years, died near Londonderry on 3 January 1780. [SM.42.53]

MCNEMARA, DENIS, aged 95, alias *Ruadh* or *Red-haired,* an Irish poet or bard, died in Newton near Kilmacthomas on 6 October 1810. [SM.72.958]

MCNIELL, JOHN, an Excise officer in Downpatrick, and his daughter Mary Ann McNiell, died in Downpatrick in May 1804. [SM.66.479]

MCOWAN, MARGARET, aged 115, died at Castle Nock on 1 October 1777. [SM.39.567]

MCPHERSON, ....., son of Dr McPherson of the 42nd [Royal Highland] Regiment, was born in Richmond Barracks, Dublin, on 12 May 1820. [SM.85.583]

MCPHERSON, ....., son of Dr McPherson of the 42nd Regiment, was born in Limerick on 13 September 1822. [SM.89.750]

MCPHERSON, ......, daughter of Lieutenant Colonel McPherson of the 78th Highlanders, was born in the Royal Barracks, Dublin, in 1825. [SM.95.254]

MAQUIRE, HUGH, late Lieutenant Colonel of Foot on the Irish Establishment, formerly an officer in Imperial service, died in Dublin in April 1766. [SM.28.223]

MACQUIRE, Lieutenant General, Colonel of a regiment of Warasdins in the service of the Empress Queen, died in Turin, 1750. [SM.12.399]

MACQUIRE, Lady, spouse of Colonel MacQuire and relict of the late Lord Cathcart, died in Ireland in April 1748. [SM.10.250]

MACQUEEN, KENNETH, son of Archibald MacQueen minister in the Isle of Skye, died in Dublin on 6 February 1750. [SM.12.205]

**MCQUOLD, Reverend EDWARD,** aged 54, parish priest of Portaferry, died on 5 October 1815. [SM.77.879]

**MCROBERTS, JOHN,** MD, second son of James McRoberts of Listoodor, County Down, married Mary Finlayson, second daughter of the late William Finlayson, Union Place, Aberdeen, in Athlone on 25 October 1819. [SM.84.487]

**MACROBERT, .....,** son and daughter of John MacRobert of the 10$^{th}$ Hussars, were born in Kilkenny on 23 November 1823. [SM.93.126]

**MCVEIGH, HENRY,** of Lurgan, married Mary Crichton, daughter of the late Robert Crichton of Auchinskeoch, in Lasswade on 6 June 1808. [SM.70.477]

**MAGEE, JOHN,** late of College Green, proprietor of the *Dublin Evening Post*, died in Dublin in 1809. [SM.71.880]

**MAGEE, Mrs,** aged 102, died in Limerick in 1790. 'She has left 74 children, grandchildren, and great-grandchildren'. [SM.53.50]

**MAGEE, .....,** eldest daughter of William Magee in Belfast, and wife of John Cumming, died in Naples on 6 January 1821. [SM.87.294]

**MAGEE, .....,** daughter of Robert Magee, was born in Dublin on 13 April 1826. [SM.97.639]

**MAGUIRE, HUGH,** son of Hugh Macquire of Drumdow, and heir to Governor Macrae, died at Schellen, France, on 8 December 1754. [SM.16.595]

**MAINAUDUE, ELIAS,** aged 80, died in Cork in 1790. 'He was one of the greatest mathematicians in

Europe, and father of the much talked of lecturer on animal magnetism.' [SM.52.311]

**MAITLAND, Reverend GEORGE,** brother to the Earl of Lauderdale, died in Ireland in September 1764. [SM.26.519]

**MAITLAND, Colonel JAMES,** of the 84$^{th}$ Regiment, married Isabella Ann Manners, eldest daughter of Thomas Manners, Clerk to the Signet, in Tritonville, Dublin, on 2 March 1824. [SM.93.511]

**MAITLAND, JOHN,** a Captain of the Royal Navy, youngest son of the late Colonel Richard Maitland, brother of the late Earl of Lauderdale, married Dora Bateman, eldest daughter of C, Bateman of Bedford, County Kerry, in Bath on 6 January 1820. [SM.85.189]

**MAITLAND, .....,** son of Captain F. Maitland of the frigate Loire, was born in Ballibricken, Ireland, on 2 December 1805. [SM.67.966]

**MALCOLMSON, SARAH,** aged 121, died at Drumgoolin on 6 April 1810. [SM.72.478]

**MALEADY, ELINOR,** aged 102, died at Newton, County Kildare, in February 1752. [SM.14.101]

**MALEY, EDWARD,** aged 110, died at Cappagnvicar near Castlebar on 17 January 1811. [SM.73.159]

**MANDEVILLE, JOHN,** aged 102, of Ballynagh, married ......Mandeville, aged 16, daughter of Thomas Mandeville, in Ballydine, County Tipperary, on 19 May 1755. [SM.17.268]

**MANN, Dr,** Bishop of Cork, died in Bath on 11 December 1788. [SM.50.623]

**MANNERS, CHARLES,** Duke of Rutland, a Lieutenant General and General Governor of Ireland, died in Dublin Castle on 24 October 1787. [SM.49.569]

**MANNERS, Lord,** Lord High Chancellor of Ireland, married Jane Butler, sister to Lord Caher, in Baron's Court, Tyrone, on 28 October 1815. [SM.77.957]

**MANNERS, .....,** son of Lady Manners, was born in Dublin on 17 August 1818. [SM.82.203]

**MAPLETOFT, Miss,** daughter of the Hon. Mrs Mapletoft, married the Right Reverend Lord Bishop of Cork, in 1791. [SM.53.514]

**MARLEY, Dr GEORGE,** Bishop of Dromore, died in Venice on 12 April 1763. [SM.25.301]

**MARSH, Reverend DIGBY,** DD, Fellow of Trinity College, Dublin, Professor of Modern History, Registrar of the University, and Member of the Royal Irish Academy, died in his chambers in Trinity College in 1791. [SM.53.467]

**MARSHALL, ANTHONY P.,** from Edinburgh, married Frances Holden, fourth daughter of the late Smollet Holden of Dublin, there on 20 August 1824. [SM.94.510]

**MARSHALL, Major JOSIAH,** in the service of the East India Company, married Catherine Babbington, eldest daughter of Reverend Dr William Babbington of Dumfries, at Bonney Glen, Ireland, on 10 October 1811. [SM.73.876]

**MARSHALL, MATTHEW,** aged 50, formerly sergeant major of the Enniskillen Dragoons, fought at the Battle of Waterloo, died in Belfast on 28 September 1825. [SM.96.639]

**MARTIN, JAMES,** aged 112, a farmer, died at Ballynahinch on 3 April 1763. 'He labored his farm till within a few years of his death, and drove his own plough through the season at 107'. [SM.25.301]

**MASON, JOHN MONCK,** aged 84, died in Dublin in 1808. [SM.71.320]

**MASON, .....,** of the Kingdom of Ireland, married Lady Betty Villers, daughter of the Earl of Grandeson, 1739. [SM.I.583]

**MASSERENE, Lord Viscount,** of Ireland, married Miss Eyre, only child of Henry Eyre, in Derby, 1741. [SM.3.523]

**MASSERENE, the Viscount Dowager,** died in Dublin on 1 July 1749. [SM.11.350]

**MASSAREENE, the Countess Dowager,** aged 89, died in Dublin on 20 May 1805. [SM.67.486]

**MASSEY, HUGH,** 2nd Lord Massey, son of Hugh created Lord Massey in 1776, died in Dublin aged 67 in 1791. He married Catherine, eldest daughter of Edward Taylor of Ballynort, by whom he had three sons and four daughters. He succeeded his father in 1788. [SM.53.152]

**MASSY, JOHN,** late MP for Limerick, died at Massy Park, Limerick, on 6 August 1815. [SM.77.875]

**MATTHEW, FRANCIS,** eldest son of Lord Viscount Landaff, married Miss G. La Touch, daughter of John La Touch, in Dublin on 11 July 1797. [SM.59.503]

**MATTHEW, THOMAS,** of Thomastown, died at the castle of Thurles in Ireland on 3 December 1777. He was succeeded by his only son Francis Mathew,

knight of the shire and Governor of Tipperary.
[SM.39.622]

**MATTHEW, Mrs,** died in Tipperary in 1781.
[SM.43.380]

**MATURIN, Reverend C. R.,** MA, Curate of St Peter's,
died in Dublin on 30 October 1824. [SM.94.768]

**MAUDE, JAMES ASHLEY,** a Captain of the Royal Navy,
married Albina Brodrick, second daughter of the
Archbishop of Cashel, in St Anne's Church, Dublin, on
18 October 1817. [SM.80.397]

**MAULE, Dr HENRY,** Bishop of Meath, died in Dublin
on 13 April 1758. He was one of the first promoters of
the Protestant charter schools in that kingdom.
[SM.20.220]

**MAULE, Mrs,** of Panmure, died at Jenny Mount near
Belfast on 11 May 1821. [SM.87.592; 88.93]

**MAURICE, Dr EDWARD,** Bishop of Ossory, died at
Dunmore, Ireland, on 4 February 1756. [SM.18.108]

**MAXWELL, Dr HENRY,** Lord Bishop of Meath, died in
Dublin in 1798. [SM.60.719]

**MAXWELL, J. A.,** a Lieutenant of the 26th Regiment of
Foot, died in Cork Barracks on 19 September 1823.
[SM.92.640]

**MAXWELL, JOHN,** Lord Farnham, an Irish peer, died
in Ireland on 15 August 1759. He was succeeded by
his son Robert Maxwell MP for Taunton. [SM.21.445]

**MAXWELL, JOHN,** eldest son of the Bishop of Meath,
married Miss Annesley, daughter of Lord Viscount
Valentia, in Dublin during 1789. [SM.51.309]

**MAXWELL, ROBERT,** Earl of Farnham in Ireland, died at his seat in Cavan on 18 October 1779. He was succeeded by his eldest brother Barry, MP for County Cavan. [SM.41.631]

**MAXWELL, Mrs,** wife of the Lord Bishop of Meath, and only sister of the House of Commons, died in Ireland in 1792. [SM.53.155]

**MAXWELL, Mrs,** wife of Lieutenant Colonel Maxwell of the Donegal Regiment of Militia, died in Drogheda in 1795. [SM.57.749]

**MAY, Sir JAMES,** of Mayfield, County Waterford, aged 91, Member of Parliament for County Waterford, died in May Park on 15November 1811. [SM.74.78]

**MAYNE, WILLIAM,** Lord Newhaven, died in Dublin on 23 May 1794. [SM.56.308]

**Mayo, .....,** son of Viscount Mayo, was born in Ireland, 1743. [SM.5.526]

**Mayo, JOHN, Lord Viscount,** of the Kingdom of Ireland, died in London on 12 January 1767. [SM.29.55]

**Mayo, Lady Viscountess,** widow of Viscount Mayo of the Kingdom of Ireland, died in London on 3 June 1794. [SM.56.374]

**Meath, the Countess of,** died at Bath on 6 December 1758. [SM.20.660]

**MELVILLE, Dr ROBERT,** M.A.[Glasgow], M.D.[Trinity College, Dublin], died in Moate, County Westmeath, on 5 September 1818. His wife died on 10 September 1818. [SM.82.391]

**MERCER, Captain WILLIAM,** aged 80, died in Dublin on 24 December 1759. 'Served under the Earl of Peterborough in Spain. [SM.21.663]

**MERCHANT, ELISABETH,** aged 133, died at Hamilton's Baun, County Armagh, on 30 November 1761. 'Her husband died about 15 years ago, in the 116th year of his age'. [SM.23.671]

**MIDDLETON, Lady,** relict of Lord Middleton the Lord Chancellor of Ireland, died in Dublin on 5 January 1748. [SM.10.50]

**MIDDLETON, ......,** son and heir to Lord Viscount Middleton, an Irish peer, was born in London on 1 November 1754. [SM.16.500]

**MIDDLETON, Lord Viscount,** of the Kingdom of Ireland, married Frances Pelham of Stanmer, Sussex, on 2 December 1778. [SM.40.686]

**MIDDLETON, .....,** son of Major Middleton of the 72nd Regiment, was born in Belfast on 5 November 1825. [SM.96.765]

**MILLAY, ......,** two boys and three girls, stillborn, children of John Millay, schoolmaster, 23 March 1779. [SM.41.221]

**MILLER, J. FITZWILLIAM,** late of the Royal Scots, married Prudence Power, daughter of the late Edward Power, in Limerick on 27 September 1817. [SM.80.294]

**MILLER, JOHN,** town major of Limerick, died 1740. [SM.2.95]

**MILLER, THOMAS HAMILTON,** an advocate, third son of Patrick Miller of Dalswinton, married Miss Ram, daughter of Abel Ram, Member of Parliament for County Wexford, on 4 April 1809. [SM.71.317]

**MILLER, .....,** daughter of Captain Miller ADC to the Commander of the Forces, was born in the Royal Hospital, Dublin, on 19 December 1816. [SM.79.79]

**MILLS, Dr,** Bishop of Waterford and Lismore, died 1740. [SM.2.238]

**MILNE, HENRY,** Lieutenant Colonel of the 93rd Highlanders, died in Dublin on 30 December 1822. [SM.91.255]

**Miltown, the Earl of,** died in Dublin on 10 January 1807. [SM.69.80]

**MITCHELL, Captain,** of the 45th Regiment, died in Cork on 16 May 1775. [SM.37.286]

**Moira, the Earl of,** aged 73, died at his seat in Ireland on 20 June 1793. [SM.55.309]

**Molesworth, ......,** son of Lord Viscount Molesworth, was born in Dublin on 4 November 1748. [SM.10.563]

**Molesworth, .......,** daughter of Viscountess Molesworth, was born in Dublin on 17 October 1751. [SM.13.455]

**MOLESWORTH, ROBERT,** son of Viscount Molesworth, married Miss Jones, daughter of Viscount Ranelagh, in Dublin in 1793. [SM.55.516]

**MOLYNEAUX, ......,** 'the celebrated pugilist', died in Galway on 4 August 1818. [SM.82.295]

**MONAGHAN, MORTOGH,** a laborer, aged 103, died at Loghboy, 2 July 1752. [SM.14.366]

**MONCK, GEORGE HENRY,** died in Dublin on 16 December 1787. [SM.50.50]

**MONCKE, HENRY,** of the Kingdom of Ireland, married Lady Arabella Bentink, sister to the Duke of Portland, 1739. [SM.I.583]

**MONCKTON, .....,** eldest son of Lord Galway, died in Paris in June 1769. [SM.31.334]

**MONEYPENNY, ......,** Lieutenant Colonel, of the 56th Regiment of Foot, married Miss Chamberlaine of Peter Street, in Dublin in November 1767. [SM.29.669]

**MONTCASHEL, Lord,** married Lady Helena Rowdon, second daughter of the Earl of Moira, in Dublin on 3 June 1769. [SM.31.334]

**MONTGOMERY, HUGH,** Earl of Mount Alexander, died in Dublin on 26 February 1745, and was succeeded by his only brother Thomas. [S.7.150]

**MONTGOMERY, HUGH,** of Castle Hume in Ireland, married Miss Acheson, daughter of Lord Gosford, in Dublin in August 1778. [SM.40.454]

**MONTGOMERY, JONATHAN,** aged 105, died in Cashel on 14 April 1784. [SM.46.223]

**MONTGOMERY, JOHN,** a merchant in Lisbon, died there on 6 November 1786. He was brother to Alexander Montgomery in Ireland and brother to the heroic General Montgomery. [SM.48.571]

**MONTGOMERY, JOHN,** eldest son of Hugh Montgomery of Benvarden, County Antrim, High Sheriff of Antrim, married Jane Ferguson, third daughter of the late Sir Andrew Ferguson of the Farm near Londonderry and niece to the Bishop of Down,

in Londonderry Cathedral on 5 March 1819.
[SM.83.384]

**MONTGOMERY, Sir WILLIAM,** of Machiehill, baronet,
died in Dublin on 25 December 1788. [SM.51.49]

**MONTGOMERY, Lady,** spouse of Sir William
Montgomery, died in Dublin on 19 June 1777.
[SM.39.335]

**MONTGOMERY, Mrs,** sister of the late and aunt of
the present Duke of Argyle, and relict of William
Montgomery of Rosemount, died in Dublin on 3
January 1786. The title of Earl of Mount Alexander
thus became extinct for want of male heirs.
[SM.48.51]

**MOORE, Reverend CHARLES,** of Monasterevan,
fourth son of Ponsonby Moore and nephew of the
Marquis of Drogheda, married Agnes Cleghorn, eldest
daughter of James Cleghorn MD physician to the
State In Ireland, in Dublin on 13 September 1815.
[SM.77.873]

**MOORE, Lord HENRY SEYMOUR,** only brother of the
Marquis of Drogheda, married Mary Parnell, second
daughter of Sir Henry Parnell MP for Queen's County,
and niece of the Marquis of Bute and Earl of Port
Arlington, on 28 September 1824. [SM.94.639]

**MOORE, Lady ISABELLA,** eldest daughter of the Earl
of Drogheda, on 22 June 1787 at Moor Abbey in
Ireland, seat of his lordship. [SM.49.361]

**MOORE, JAMES,** an attorney at law, died at
Cloverhill, County Antrim, by a shooting accident, on
24 October 1797. [SM.59.783]

**MOORE, STEPHEN,** Earl and Viscount Mountcashel, Baron Kilworth, and a Privy Councillor, died in Dublin on 21 May 1790. He married Lady Helen Rawdon, second daughter of the Earl of Moira in 1769, and had three sons and a daughter. [SM.52.259]

**MOORE, Lord,** eldest son of the Earl of Drogheda, died in Toulouse, France, in August 1752. [SM.14.462]

**MOORE, .....,** a woman aged 120, died near Enniskillen on 7 December 1764/ [SM.26.687]

**MARAN, ANTHONY,** aged 108, died in Laghel near Castlebar in 1814. [SM.76.400]

**MORE, CHARLES MCCARTHY,** Captain of the 1$^{st}$ Regiment of Guards, died at Putney Common on 13 March 1770. 'He was lineally descended from Dermot McCarthy, King of Cork and Desmond in the time of Henry II'. [SM.32.167]

**MORECROFT, THOMAS,** died in Dublin, 1741. [SM.3.331]

**MORGAN, Mrs ELEANOR,** aged 105, died in Dublin on 22 December 1754. [SM.16.596]

**Mornington, Lord,** an Irish peer, married Miss Hill, daughter of Arthur Hill a Commissioner of Revenue in Ireland, in Dublin on 30 January 1759. [SM.21.100]

**Mornington, the Earl of,** of the Kingdom of Ireland, died in Kensington on 22 May 1781. [SM.43.279]

**MOSSE, Captain THOMAS,** of the 1$^{st}$ [Royal Scots] Regiment, married Margaret Essex Gordon, eldest daughter of Major General Gordon, in Cork on 16 May 1818. [SM.81.596]

**MORRIS, Lady,** relict of Sir William Morris baronet, and mother of Sir W. E. R. Morris, died in Upperwood, County Kilkenny, on 18 March 1811. [SM.73.319]

**MORRISON,......,** son of Major Morrison of the 7th Dragoon Guards, was born in Kilkenny on 18 August 1817. [SM.80.192]

**MOTLEY, Mrs CATHERINE,** aged 112, died in Kilkenny on 16 January 1769. [SM.31.54]

**Mount Alexander, the Countess of,** died in Donaghadee on 22 August 1771. [SM.33.446]

**Mount Cashel, the Countess Dowager,** died in St Stephen's Green, Dublin, on 3 June 1792. [SM.53.310]

**Mount Cashel, ......,** son and heir of the Earl of Mount Cashel, was born in Dublin on 20 August 1792. [SM.92.413]

**Mount Cashel, ........,** daughter of the Earl of Mount Cashel, was born in Dublin in 1793. [SM.55.360]

**Mountflorence, ......,** son and heir to Lord Mountflorence, was born in Ireland in March 1768. [SM.30.223]

**Mountflorence, Lady Dowager,** of Florence Court in Ireland, died in Bath on 22 April 1771. [SM.33.221]

**Mountgarret, ......,**son of Lord Viscount Mountgarret, was born in Dublin on 5 August 1754. [SM.16.404]

**Mountgarret, ......,** daughter of Lord Viscount Mountgarret, was born in Dublin on 25 August 1759. [SM.59.444]

**Mountgarret, Viscountess,** died in Paris in March 1778. [SM.40.221]

**Mountjoy, the Countess Dowager,** aged 80, died at Loughboy 29 December 1746. [SM.9.49]

**Mountmorres, HARVEY,** Lord Viscount, died in Dublin on 6 April 1766. [SM.28.223]

**Mountmorres, Viscountess,** aged 48, died in Glasnevin near Dublin on 21 July 1823. [SM.92.384]

**MOUNTNEY, RICHARD,** second baron of the Exchequer in Ireland, married the Countess Dowager of Mount Alexander, in Dublin on 2 October 1759. [SM.21.557]; he died at Belturbet, County Cavan, in March 1768. [SM.30.223]

**MOUNTSANDFORD, Lady CATHERINE,** aged 56, relict of Lord Mount Sandford, died near Dublin on 19 October 1818. [SM.82.487]

**MOVAN, HUGH,** aged 113, a soldier, died in the Royal Hospital, Dublin, on 1 May 1773. 'he served in all King William and Queen Anne's wars, continued in the army till 1726, then discharged'. [SM.35.278]

**MULEERY, DANIEL,** aged 127, died in County Sligo in April 1775. 'he fought at the Battles of Aboyne and Antrim and was wounded at both'. [SM.37.223]

**MULGRAVE, Lord CONSTANTINE JOHN,** Baron of New Ross in Ireland, died in Liege on 10 October 1792. He was succeeded in his Irish peerage by his brother Henry Phipps, Member of Parliament for Scarborough. [SM.53.519]

**MULHOLLAND, Mrs JEAN,** aged 105, aunt to Richard Magennis Member of Parliament for the Irish borough of Bangor, died in Lurgan, County Armagh, in 1788. [SM.50.416]

**MULVIHILL, GEORGE,** aged 23, from County Clare, a student of medicine in Edinburgh, died there on 3 June 1809. [SM.71.479]

**MURGATROD, Dr,** died at Kells in November 1754. [SM.16.595]

**MURPHY, ANDREW,** aged 85, died at his seat in County Wexford, on 3 April 1761. 'This estate has been handed down regularly from father to son for upwards of 1500 years'. [SM.23.222]

**MURPHY, Mrs ARTHUR,** aged 29, author of 'The Conquest of Quebec', died in Sea View, County Wexford, on 16 June 1795. [SM.57.411]

**MURPHY, EDWARD,** aged 110, steward to Sir William Parsons, died at Birr, King's County, on 8 July 1759. [SM.21.387]

**MURPHY, PATRICK,** aged 116 years, died in Limerick on 5 February 1789. 'He served as a soldier in many wars at the beginning of the present century'. [SM.51.103]

**MURRAY, JAMES,** Civil Engineer of the Royal Canal in Dublin, died in Mullingar on 19 March 1807. [SM.69.317]

**MURRAY, JOHN,** Dean of Killaloe and Rector of Castle Connel, died on 18 June 1790. 'He was uncle to the Duke of Athol and married Lady Elizabeth Murray, sister to the Earl of Dunmore, by whom he had two daughters.' [SM.52.310]

**MURRAY, MAGDALENE,** eldest daughter of David Murray in Dundalk, married Robert Haig from London, in Dundalk Church on 1 November 1823. [SM.92.766]

**MURRAY, WILLIAM,** married Catherine Hamilton, second daughter of Viscount Boyne, in Ireland in January 1769. [SM.31.54]

**MURRAY, Dr.,** born in County Clare, an eminent physician in Paris, died there on 9 January 1767. [SM.29.55]

**MURRAY, ......,** son of Lady Charlotte MacGregor Murray, was born in Kinsale on 19 February 1811. [SM.73.236]

**MURRAY,......,** son of Lieutenant Colonel Murray, was born in Athlone on 19 February 1819. [SM.83.284]

**MURRAY, ......,** son of Henry Murray, was born in Douglas near Cork on 21 February 1820. [SM.85.388]

**MUSGRAVE, Sir RICHARD,** baronet, Excise Collector for the port of Dublin, died in Dublin in 1818. [SM.81.500]

**MUSKERRY, Baron,** Governor and Custos Rotulorum of County Limerick, and Colonel of the County Limerick Militia, died in Springfield, near Charleville, County Cork, on 25 June 1818. [SM.82.295]

**MUTER, ROBERT,** a Captain of the 7th Royal Fusiliers, married Fanny O'Neill, eldest daughter of John O'Neill of Lanch Hill, County Dublin, on 7 January 1820. [SM.85.188]

**MYLNE, WILLIAM,** architect and chief engineer of Dublin, died in Dublin on 6 March 1790. 'He was a member of the Corporations of Masons in Edinburgh, convenor of the trades in 1765, and built the North Bridge in that city. His ancestors have been masons from father to son in Edinburgh some hundreds of years, one of whom built the Palace of Holyroodhouse.' [SM.52.154]

**NAPIER, General,** Governor of the hospitals and Lieutenant-General of the forces in Ireland, died 1739. [SM.I.583]

**NAPIER, Lieutenant Colonel FRANCIS,** commanding officer of the Marines, died in Dublin on 30 June 1780. [SM.42.389]

**NAPIER, JEAN MACDOWALL,** wife of William Augustus Kellet a banker in Cork, and daughter of the deceased Colonel William Napier of Culcreuch, died in Cork on 2 October 1805. [SM.67.807]

**NAPIER, ......,** daughter of Lord Napier, was born in Cork on 9 September 1785. [SM.47.467]

**NAPIER, .......,** son of Lord Napier, was born in Kinsale on 13 October 1786. [SM.48.517]

**NAPIER, ......,** son of Captain Napier of the 63rd Regiment of Foot, was born in Wexford on 27 September 1792. [SM.53.518]

**NEAL, DARBY,** aged 117, a laborer, died at Skibbereen near Dingle, on 12 December 1767. [SM.29.670]

**NEDHAM, GEORGE,** of Down in Ireland, nephew to the Earl of Chatham, and MP for Newry, died in London on 12 December 1769. [SM.29.670]

**NEEDHAM, THOMAS,** a banker, died in Dublin on 4 January 1806. [SM.67.79]

**NEILSON, Reverend WILLIAM,** aged 46, Professor of Latin, Greek, and Hebrew at the Classical School of the Belfast Institution, died in Belfast on 26 May 1821. [SM.87.591]

**NESBIT, JOHN,** of Kineghan, County Meath, married Mary Laidlow, daughter of the late Walter Laidlow of Hundleshop, in Edinburgh in 1788. [SM.50.154]

**NETHERTON, .....,** aged 110, died in Dublin on 26 January 1756. 'He was a trise Inniskilliner and served under King William in the wars in Ireland.' [SM.18.51]

**NEVIL, Lieutenant General CLEMENT,** a Major General on the Irish establishment, also a Colonel of a regiment of horse, died in Dublin on 5 August 1744. [SM.6.395]

**NEWALL, JOHN,** aged 127, died in Michaelstown, County Cork, on 25 July 1761. 'He was grandson to old Parr of England who lived to the age of 152 years'. [SM.23.391]

**Newbattle, Lord,** son of the Earl of Ancrum, married Miss Fortescue, niece to the Earl of Mornington, in Ireland in June 1762. [SM.24.349]

**Newbattle, ......,**son of Lord Newton, son of the Earl of Ancrum, was born in Dublin on 4 October 1763. [SM.25.583]

**NEWCOMBE, Reverend Dr WILLIAM,** Archbishop of Armagh and Primate of Ireland, died in Dublin on 12 January 1800. [SM.62.71]

**NEWCOMEN, Sir WILLIAM GLEADOWE,** baronet, 'principal of the oldest banking house in Ireland', died in Killester House near Dublin on 21 August 1807. [SM.69.799]

**NEWPORT, SIMON,** born 11 November 1727, an alderman of Waterford, died there on 7 December 1817. [SM.81.95]

**NEWPORT, Lady,** wife of the Lord Chancellor of Ireland, died in Dublin on 23 February 1748. [SM.10.153]

**NEWPORT, Lord,** Lord Chancellor of Ireland, married Lady Dowager Ross, in Dublin on 15 November 1754. [SM.16.548]

**NEWTON, .....,** son of Lady Viscountess Newton, was born in Dublin on 29 September 1761. [SM.23.558]

**NOBLE, ANTHONY,** aged 115, gardener to Henry Bevan of Milltown, Ireland, died in 1790 aged 115. 'He worked in his garden till within five or six days of his death'. [SM.52.258]

**NOON, or MOONEY, CATHERINE,** aged 116, died near Tuam on 8 June 1768. Her husband died a few years previously aged 128 leaving numerous offspring. [SM.30.335]

**NOON, JOHN,** aged 129, of County Galway, died 27 February 1762. [SM.24.112]

**NORRIS, JAMES,** late Lieutenant Colonel of De Jean's Dragoons, died in Dublin on 21 June 1756. [SM.18.314]

**NORTH, JOHN HENRY,** a barrister-at-law, married Letitia Dorothy Foster, youngest daughter of the late Bishop of Clogher, in Dublin on 3 December 1818. [SM.83.94]

**Northland, Lord Viscount,** died at Dungannon Park on 5 December 1818. [SM.83.96]

**NORTON, Mrs,** aged 109, died at Athy, County Kildare, 1761. 'About five years ago, she led a country dance at the wedding of one of her great grandchildren, where 42 of her offspring were present'. [SM.23.335]

**NUGENT, HENRY EDMOND,** aged 8, second son of the Earl of West Meath, died in Dublin on 3 March 1811. [SM.73.318]

**NUGENT, IGNATIUS,** of Finglas, grandson of Richard, Earl of West Meath, died in March 1773. 'he has left three sons, two of whom served all the last war in Germany, one as a Captain, the other as a Lieutenant, in the 2oth Regiment of Foot'. [SM.35.278]

**NUGENT, ROBERT CRAGGS,** aged 87, Viscount Clare and Earl Nugent in Ireland, father of the present Marchioness of Buckingham, died in Dublin in 1788. [SM.50.570]

**NUGENT, THOMAS,** Earl of Westmeath, Viscount and Baron Delvin, a Privy Councillor of Ireland, one of the original Knight Companions of the most illustrious Order of St Patrick, and chief of the Nugents, died in Dublin on 7 September 1792. 'He was the first Earl of Westmeath of the Protestant religion, having conformed in 1755. He was succeeded by his only son George Frederick, Lord Delvin.' [SM.53.466]

**O'BRIAN, CHARLOTTE,** daughter of the late Sir Lucius O'Brian baronet, of Dromoland, County Clare, married Gerrard Noel, son of Colonel Noel the Member of Parliament for Rutlandshire, in Dublin on 15 February 1806. [SM.67.237]

**O'BRIAN, DANIEL,** aged 76, 'styling himself Earl of Lismore in Ireland, died in Rome on 5 November

1759. One of the Chevalier de St George's ministers'. [SM.21.663]

O'BRIAN, Captain EDWARD, brother of Sir Lucius O'Brian, baronet, and brother-in-law to the Countess of Charlemont, died in Ireland in 1787. [SM.49.622]

O'BRIAN, HANNAH, born in Ireland in 1647, died in a village near Chester on 10 November 1757. [SM.19.669]

O'BRIAN, HENRY, Earl of Thomond, died in Dublin on 20 April 1741. [SM.3.191]

O'BRIAN, JAMES, aged 114, died in Carrickfergus in October 1780. 'He served as a paymaster-sergeant in the wars in Ireland, in the reign of James II]. [SM.42.673]

O'BRIAN, JAMES, 'the famous Irish giant', died in Cork in July 1804. [SM.66.647]

O'BRIAN, Mrs MARY, wife of Patrick O'Brian, an authoress and poet, died in Dublin on 17 June 1790. [SM.52.310]

O'BRIAN, PATRICK, aged 114, a carpenter, died in Meath in August 1758. [SM.20.443]

O'BRIAN, PATRICK COTTER, born in Kinsale in 1760, his stature was 8 foot 1 inch, died at Hotwells, Bristol, on 8 September 1806. He belonged to the Masonic Order of Knights Templar, and was buried in the Catholic Chapel in Trenchard Street, Bristol. [SM.67.727]

O'BRIAN, PAUL, aged 107, a cooper, died in Asolas, County Clare, in 1786. [SM.48.465]

**O'BURNE, .....,** the Irish giant, married Mary Anne Colston of Merton Sea End near Spalding at Wisbech on 11 September 1784. 'There were upwards of 1500 persons to celebrate the nuptials'. [SM.46.503]

**O'CARROL, Sir DANIEL,** died in Dublin on 3o January 1758. [SM.20.161]

**O'CONNOR, DANIEL,** aged 92, died in Brussels, he was a Lieutenant Field Marshal of the Empress Queen's forces, and had been 61 years in the service of Austria and Lorraine. [SM.18.108]

**O'CONNOR, DENNIS,** 'a direct descendant of the Kings of that name, and brother of the Irish historian', died in Ballinagare, County Roscommon, on 6 July 1804. [SM.66.727]

**O'CONNOR, PATRICK,** aged 104, died in Carrickfergus in September 1783. [SM.45.560]

**O'CONNOR, THOMAS,** brother of the late Dominick O'Connor Don of Cloonalis, and of Alexander O'Connor Don, lineal male descendant of Roderick O'Connor Don, King of Connaught, and Monarch of Ireland, died in Armhouse, County Roscommon, in October 1817. [SM.81.95]

**O'DONNELL, CHARLES,** aged 76, Roman Catholic Bishop of Derry, died there on 18 July 1823. [SM.92.256]

**O'DONNEL, HUGH,** died at Belturbet, Ireland, during November 1754. [SM.16.595]

**O'DONNEL, Count,** aged 102, born in Ireland, formerly an officer in Hungarian service, died in Brussels on 13 September 1767. [SM.29.501]

**O'DONNEL, Count,** formerly Commandant of the Irish Regiment in French service, and a Knight of St Louis, died in Paris on 3 June 1789. [SM.51.361]

**O'GRADY, DENNIS,** aged 106, in Thurles, County Tipperary, died 1793. [SM.55.101]

**O'HALLORAN, SYLVESTER,** aged 85, an eminent surgeon and historian, died in Limerick in 1807. [SM.69.720]

**O'HARA, KEANE,** author of the songs in 'Thom Thumb', and the celebrated burlettas of 'Midas', the 'Golden Pippin', and the 'Misers', died in Ireland in 1782. [SM.44.334]

**O'HARA, CHARLES,** MP for Sligo, died at Nymphsfield, County Sligo, on 12 September 1822. [SM.90.632]

**O'HARA, Mrs,** aged 112, died in Drogheda on 14 August 1762. [SM.24.451]

**O'KELLY, DENNIS,** died on 28 December 1787, 'he was well known in the sporting line', 'his fortune was left to his nephew Andrew Dennis O'Kelly. [SM.49.623]

**O'KELLY, Count,** aged 103, a native of Ireland who, for many years, was in the service of the Queen of Hungary, died in Turin in October 1766. [SM.28.558]

**O'KELLY, ......,** of Aghrim, chief of the ancient and noble family of O'Kelly, died in County Roscommon, on 8 December 1767. [SM.29.670]

**O'LOUGHLIN, Mrs,** aged 108, wife of Bryan O'Loughlin, died in Limerick in 1789. [SM.51.363]

**O'MARA, TIMOTHY,** aged 100, died at Birr in Ireland, on 25 July 1762. 'He was a trooper in King William's army at the Battle of the Boyne'. [SM.24.451]

**O'MEARA, Lieutenant General DANIEL,** died in Thames Street, Limerick, on 8 August 1821. [SM.88.296]

**O'NEALE, Don CARLOS FELIX,** aged 110, died in Madrid on 10 September 1791. He was a Lieutenant General in Spanish Service, former Governor of Havannah, son of Sir Neil O'Neale of Ulster who died at the Battle of the Boyne. [SM.53.517]

**O'NEALE, HARRIOT FRANCES,** wife of John O'Neale of Slaines Castle, Ireland, died at Caldas de Rainha in Portugal on 3 September 1793. [SM.55.516]

**O'NEIL, ARTHUR,** Professor of the Irish Harp, aged 90, died in Maynooth, County Armagh, in 1816. [SM.78.960]

**O'NEIL, Sir HENRY,** aged 85, died at his seat near Drogheda on 1 November 1759. [SM.21.606]

**O'NEIL, JOHN,** of Slanes Castle in Ireland, married Miss Boyle, daughter of the late Lord Viscount Dungarvan, and niece to the Earl of Cork, in London on 18 October 1777. [SM.39.567]

**O'NEIL, JOHN,** Viscount O'Neil, died at Lord Massareene's Castle in Ireland on 16 July 1798. 'His own park-keeper wounded him with a pike, of which he died'. [SM.60.508]

**O'NEIL, PATRICK,** was born in 1647, he was married to his first wife on 18 August 1675, to his second 9 July 1684, to his third 4 May 1689, to his fourth 8 March 1701, to his fifth 5 June 1720, to his sixth 9

October 1740, and to his seventh 15 September 1760 in Clonmel. His seventh wife was of the family of O'Connor. He enlisted as a dragoon during the reign of King Charles II and remained a soldier until 1740. [SM.22.502]

**O'NIEL, .......,** an Irish linen dealer, married Mrs Marths Hartley a widow, in Whitehaven on 29 December 1794. 'On the following Monday following her husband died; so the bride has been a wife, and twice a widow in the space of a week'. [SM.57.67]

**O'REILLY, Reverend Dr.,** Catholic Archbishop of Armagh, died in Drogheda on 9 February 1818. [SM.81.296]

**O'ROURKE, Count,** died in London on 24 March 1785. He was descended from the sovereigns of Leitrim. Oliver Cromwell had stripped the family of their estate. The Count had been in Imperial and in French service and had received the order of St Louis from the King of France for his bravery. [SM..47.155]

**O'SULLIVAN, FLORENCE,** aged 111, died in Beerhaven, Ireland, on 5 April 1807. 'he has left 215 nephews and nieces'. [SM.69.398]

**O'SULLIVAN, THEODORE,** aged 115, 'the celebrated Irish bard', died in the parish of Aiglish near Killarney in 1820.[SM.85.488]

**Offory, ......,** daughter of the Earl of Offory, was born in London on 24 January 1770. [SM.31.111]

**ORAM, WILLIAM HENRY,** of the Royal Scots Greys, married Anne Ball, daughter of John Ball of Shannon, County Donegal, in Dublin on 10 May 1823. [SM.92.127]

**Orkney and Inchiquin, the Countess of,** died in Rostellan, County Cork, in 1790. Her Scottish titles went to her daughter Lady Mary, wife of Thomas Fitzmaurice, brother of the Marquis of Lansdown, and has issue a son now Lord Kirkwall. [SM.52.258]

**ORMSBY, MARY LETITIA,** daughter of the late H. M. Ormsby of Rock-savage, County Roscommon, married Captain J. G. Cowell of the Royals, in Cheltenham on 5 August 1821. [SM.88.293]

**ORR, .....,** son of John Orr a Lieutenant of the 94th Regiment, was born on 19 February 1818 at Richmond Barracks, Dublin. [SM.81.294]

**OSBORNE, Sir THOMAS,** died near Clonmell in 1821. [SM.88.96]

**OSWALD, Dr JOHN,** Bishop of Raphoe, died in Raphoe on 5 March 1780. [SM.42.166]

**PAKENHAM, MICHAEL,** Lord Longford, a Privy Councillor of Ireland, an a captain in the navy, died at his seat in Ireland on 6 June 1792. He married Catherine, daughter of Hercules Langford Rowley in July 1768 and had five sons and five daughters of whom Thomas the eldest, born 1774, succeeds to the titles and estates. [SM.53.310]

**PAKENHAM, THOMAS,** who was created Baron Longford in 1754, died at his seat of Longford in Ireland on 30 April 1766. [SM.28.335]

**PALLISSER, THOMAS,** aged 107, died in Portobello, County Wexford, on 16 November 1756. ' He served as an officer in all the wars under King William'. [SM.18.573]

**PALMER, Lady ELEANOR,** aged 98, relict of Sir Roger Palmer of Castle Lacken, County Mayo, and Ballyshannon, County Kildare, died in Abbey Street, Dublin, on 3 February 1818. [SM.81.296]

**PALMER, GEORGE,** of Rahine, County Kildare, aged 102, died in Waterford on 11 December 1813. [SM.76.158]

**PARKER, GERVACE,** a Lieutenant of the British Fusiliers, Fort Major of Kinsale, died 1739. [SM.I.375]

**PARKHILL, Mrs ELIZABETH,** wife of Hugh Henderson late of Glasgow, died in Ballymore Eustace in Ireland, on 24 April 1789. [SM.51.205]

**PARR, CATHARINE,** aged 103, great grand-daughter of Thomas Parr of England, died in Skiddy's Almshouse in Cork on 1 November 1792. [SM.54..571]

**PARR, Captain,** aged 107, died in Dublin on 30 December 1764. [SM.27.55]

**PARSLEY, JOSIAS,** aged 107, died in County Wicklow, 1739. [SM.I.484]

**PARSONS, RICHARD,** Earl of Ross in Ireland, died 1741. [SM.3.331]

**PATERSON, WILLIAM,** MD, an eminent physician in Derry, died in May 1807. [SM.69.479]

**PATISON, Major ANDREW,** of the 29th Regiment, died in Belfast on 11 October 1821. [SM.88.496]

**PAYNE, Brigadier General,** married Miss Quin, daughter of Lord Adair, in Dublin in 1804. [SM.66.971]

**PEACOCK, Dr,** physician to the army in Ireland, died on the 30 August 1744. [SM.6.395]

**PEARCE, Lieutenant Colonel CHARLES WILLIAM,** 'the oldest officer in British service', died in Ireland on 6 February 1775. [SM.37.110]

**PENDAR, MICHAEL,** aged 107, died in Ballynure, near Clones, in 1817. 'He had been a pensioner for 72 years'. [SM.80.502]

**PERCIVAL, JOHN,** Earl of Egmont, an Irish peer, died in London on 4 December 1770. [SM.32.684]

**PETTY, JOHN,** Earl of Sherburn in Ireland, died near Calne in Wiltshire, on 14 May 1761. 'He is succeeded in title and estate by his son Lord Fitzmaurice'. [SM.23.280]

**PHELAN, .....,** four children of Daniel Phelan a laborer, were born in Dunmore, County Waterford, on 15 November 1816. [SM.78.957]

**PHELLAN, JOHN,** aged 112, a tinker, 'he earned his bread till he was 106'. [SM.18.253]

**PHILPOT, ......,** quads, children of Mr Philpot, a farmer in Arklow, were born in May 1777. [SM.39.279]

**PHIPPS, CONSTANTINE,** Baron Mulgrave, of the Kingdom of Ireland, died at the Spa on 13 September 1775. 'he has left one son, Constantine Phipps now Lord Mulgrave, who enjoys a fortune of £16,000 per annum'. [SM.37.525]

**PIERSON, Captain THOMAS,** died near Kilbeggan, County West Meath, in October 1753. 'He served in all the campaigns under the Duke of Marlborough'. [SM.15.581]

**PLACE, CAROLINE,** daughter of Alexander Place in Dublin, married Donald Cameron a Captain of the Aberdeenshire militia, in Musselburgh on 9 November 1808. [SM.70.877]

**PLUNKET, CHARLOTTE,** sister of Lord Cloncurry and wife of Edward son of Lord Dunsany, died in Pisa in 1818. [SM.82.392]

**PLUNKET, MARGARET,** eldest daughter of Lord Dunsany, married Lord Louth in 1808. [SM.70.637]

**PLUNKET, Reverend THOMAS,** eldest son of William C. Plunket, married Louisa Jane Foster, second daughter of the late John William Foster, at Castle Bellingham, Ireland, on 26 October 1819. [SM.84.487]

**PLUNKET, Dr** an eminent physician, died in Dublin on 9 May 1809. [SM.71.400]

**PLUNKETT, ......,** child of Matthew Plunkett, was born at Greenwood Lodge, Wicklow, on 22 February 1815. [SM.77..317]

**PLUNKETT, Mrs,** wife of W. C. Plunkett, died at St Stephen's Green, Dublin, on 25 March 1821. [SM.87.495]

**POCOCKE, Dr RICHARD,** Bishop of Meath, died in Ireland on 25 September 1765. [SM.27.502]

**POMEROY, JOHN,** aged 66, Lieutenant General of H.M. Forces, Colonel of the 64th Regiment of Foot, Member of Parliament for Trim, and a Privy Councillor, died in Dublin on 10 June 1790. [SM.52.310]

**PONSONBY, BRABAZON,** aged 81, Earl of Besborough in Ireland, and Lord Ponsonby of Sysonby,

Leicestershire, England, died at his seat in County Kilkenny on 4 July 1758. [SM.20.390]

**PONSONBY, CHAMBRAY BRABAZON,** Member of the Irish Parliament, married Lady Harriot Taylor, eldest daughter of the Earl of Bective, on 4 June 1791. [SM.53.306]

**PONSONBY, JOHN,** died at Bishop's Court, County Kildare, on 16 August 1787. He was Member of Parliament for the borough of Newtown in County Down, a trustee of the linen manufacture, a member of the Dublin Society, and a Privy Councillor, Speaker of the Irish House of Commons. [SM.49.467]

**PONSONBY, WILLIAM,** Earl of Besborough, Viscount Duncannon, Baron of Besborough in Ireland, Baron Ponsonby of Sysonby in England, died on 11 March 1793 aged 82. [SM.55.154]

**PONSONBY, .....,** daughter of Lord Ponsonby, was born in Dublin in January 1750. [SM.12.54]

**POPE, THOMAS,** Lieutenant Colonel of the 2$^{nd}$ Regiment of Horse, died in Dublin in September 1775. [SM.37.526]

**Portarlington, JOHN, Earl of,** Colonel of the Royal Regiment of the Queen's County Militia, died at Auchnacloy, Ireland, in 1798. [SM.60.864]

**PORTER, JOHN,** an alderman of Dublin, died 1739. [SM.I.332]

**PORTER, ......,** two daughter of James Porter, were born in Tramore on 28 March 1805. [SM.67.325]

**PORTER, Reverend Dr.,** Bishop of Clogher, died in Clogher Palace on 27 July 1819. [SM.83.295]

**PORTEUS, WILLIAM,** aged 96, died in Leghorn, Louth, Ireland, in 1817. [SM.80.196]

**POWER, Lord HENRY,** died in Dublin on 5 May 1742. [SM.5.242]

**Powerscourt, Lord Viscount,** married Lady Frances Theodosia Jocelyn, eldest daughter of the Earl of Rosen, at Dundalk House on 6 February 1813. [SM.75.237]

**POWERSCROFT, Lord Viscount,** married Lady Catherine Meade, second daughter of the Earl of Clanwilliam, on 1 July 1789 in Dublin. [SM.51.361]

**Powerscourt, ......,** son of Lord Viscount Powerscourt, was born in Powerscourt House, Wicklow, on 17 January 1815. [SM.77.236]

**PRATT, Reverend JOSEPH,** aged 84, died at his seat in Cabra Castle, County Cavan, on 7 August 1792. Mrs Pratt, his relict, also aged 84, died a few days later. 'They had been married about 60 years'. [SM.53.414]

**PRATT, Miss,** eldest daughter of Joseph Pratt of Cabra Castle in Ireland, 'with a fortune of £100,000 ', married Charles Morton, MD, principal librarian of the British Museum, on 26 April 1791. [SM.53.257]

**PRATT, Lieutenant,** of the 5th Regiment, died in Cork 1808. [SM.70.560]

**PRESCOT, Dr RICHARD,** aged 111, died near Edenberry, King's County, in 1784. [SM.46.663]

**PRESTON, JOHN,** Member of Parliament for Navan borough, and nephew to the Earl of Ludlow, died in Edinburgh on 19 January 1781. [SM.43.110]

**PRESTON, Right Reverend WILLIAM,** Bishop of Leighlin and Ferns, died in Dublin during 1789. [SM.51.207]

**PRICE, Dr ARTHUR,** Archbishop of Cashel, died in Dublin on 17 July 1752. [SM.14.366]

**PRICE, NICHOLAS,** Lieutenant Governor of Kinsale, died there on 29 May 1776. [SM.38.340]

**PRICE, ......,** daughter of R. L. Price and his wife the Countess of Desert, was born in Desert, County Kilkenny, in 1825. [SM.95.255]

**PRIMROSE, GILBERT,** a Lieutenant Colonel on the Irish Establishment, died 1739. [SM.I.376]

**PROBY, Lady EMMA ELISABETH,** eldest daughter of the Earl of Carysfort, died in Dublin on 29 June 1791. [SM.53.309]

**PURDON, WILLIAM JOHN,** from Dublin, died in Chester on 31 May 1793. [SM.55.307]

**QUEADE, Lady GRACE,** daughter of James, Earl of Aldborough, and sister of the present Earl, died in Dublin in 1803. [SM.65.363]

**QUIG, .......,** triplets, were born to Richard Quig, an apprentice ropemaker in Londonderry, and his wife Mary, on 22 June 1811. [SM.73.635]

**QUINN, CHARLES WILLIAM,** 'for 30 years physician-general to HM Forces in Ireland', died at Ballyornan, County Wicklow, in 1819. [SM.83.288]

**RAEBURN, JOHN,** architect and clerk of works in Downpatrick, died there on 18 July 1825. [SM.96.383]

**RAINSFORD, THOMAS,** Lieutenant Colonel of Waldegrave's Regiment of Foot, died in Cork on 10 September 1754. [SM.16.451]

**RAITE, GEORGE,** a Captain of the 72nd Regiment of Foot, married Eliza Gordon, daughter of Thomas Gordon of Spring Gardens, in Clonmell in 1804. [SM.66.478]

**RAMSAY, Mrs HELEN,** spouse of Alexander Stronach of Knock, died there on 5 March 1791. [SM.53.154]

**RAWDON, JOHN THEOPHILIUS,** brother to the Earl of Moira, died in Vienna in 1808. [SM.70.477[

**RAVERTY, EDWARD,** aged 105, died in True, County Tyrone, in 1810. [SM.72.880]

**RAYBOURNE, WILLIAM,** of Enniskeen, County Cavan, aged 28, married .... Marlow, a widow aged 107. 'He is her eighth husband.' [SM.19.325]

**REDFOORD, WALTER,** born in Roxburghshire, settled in Dublin around 1762, died 'at a very advanced age' in Dublin during 1812. [SM.74.399]

**REILLY, HUGH,** aged 103, died at Mount Reilly near Dundalk in 1791. [SM.53.362]

**REILLY, ......,** three sons and a daughter, were born to James Reilly, a laborer, in St Doulas, County Dublin, on 3 November 1764. [SM.26.631]

**REILLY, ......,** three sons of John Reilly were born in Dublin on 1 January 1755. [SM.17.52]

**REVEL, ......,** a woman aged 27, died in Wexford in 1787. 'Her disease was dropsy and she had been tapped 111 times, in the course of which operations she discharged 9 barrels, 23 gallons, and 3 pints of water'. [SM.49.467]

**REYNELL, Dr CAREW,** Bishop of Derry, died in Dublin on 7 January 1745. [SM.7.50]

**REYNELL, WILLIAM,** in Ireland, married Miss Montgomery, daughter of the late Sir William Montgomery of Macheehill, baronet, on 1 July 1791. [SM.53.360]

**REYNOLDS, HENRY,** aged 103, died in Kilkenny in 1803. [SM.65.884]

**RIACH, ......,** son of Lieutenant of the 78th Highlanders, was born at Cullen, County Tipperary, on 1 January 1823. [SM.91.254]

**RICH, Sir ROBERT,** Governor of Londonderry and Culmore Fort in Ireland, died in London on 1 February 1768. [SM.30.55]

**RICHARDSON, Reverend WILLIAM,** DD, aged 80, Rector of Glonfeckle and formerly a senior Fellow of Trinity College, Dublin, died on 13 June 1820. [SM.86.191]

**RICHBELL, Major General EDWARD,** Colonel of the 17th Regiment of Foot, died in Dublin on 14 February 1757. [SM.19.111]

**RICE, THOMAS,** eldest son of Stephen Edward Rice of Mount Trenchard, Ireland, married Lady Theodosia Pery, second daughter of the Earl of Limerick, in London on 18 July 1811. [SM.73.636]

**Richmond, ......,** daughter of the Duke of Richmond, was born at the Vice Regal Lodge, Phoenix Park, Dublin, on 21 July 1809. [SM.71.639]

**RIDER, JOHN,** of Greenhills, aged 110, died in County Dublin on 23 December 1761. [SM.24.55]

**RIDGEWAY, WILLIAM,** a barrister at law, died in Dublin on 30 August 1817. [SM.80.195]

**RIGGS, EDWARD,** a Customs Commissioner in Scotland, died in Dublin, 1741. [SM.3.523]

**Riverdale, Lord,** of Ireland, died in Spring Gardens, Charing Cross, in 1787. [SM.49.622]

**RIVERS, Captain Sir JAMES,** of the 3$^{rd}$ Dragoon Guards, was accidently killed when on a shooting party near Enniskillen on 4 October 1805. [SM.67.807]

**ROBERTSON, Captain JOHN,** of the Royal Highlanders, only brother of James Robertson of Lude, Perthshire, died in Galway on 28 May 1773. [SM.35.278]

**ROBINSON, Dr BRYAN,** senior, Professor of Physics at Dublin University, died in Dublin on 26 January 1754. [SM.16.108]

**ROBINSON, GEORGE,** died in Dublin on 2 September 1790 of a wound received in a duel. [SM.52.464]

**ROBINSON, Justice,** Judge of the Court of King's Bench in Ireland, died in Dublin on 12 January 1787. [SM.49.51]

**ROCHE, Sir BOYLE,** baronet, an officer at the Siege of Havannah and later a Member of Parliament, died in Dublin in 1807. [SM.69.479]

**ROCHEFORT, Major HENRY,** aged 72, died in George's Street, Cork, on 24 October 1816. [SM.78.953]

**ROCHFORD, Mr,** died in Clontarff, Dublin, in November 1772. [SM.34.695]

**ROCK, A.,** late of the Theatre Royal in Dublin, died there on 5 November 1815. [SM.77.959]

**ROGERS, JAMES,** aged about 31, died at Ross, County Wexford, in February 1748.'who was of prodigious bulk, that though four men and a woman lay in his coffin with ease, and the lid on them, they were forced to open him and take six stones of fat from him before they could put him in'. [SM.10.102]

**ROGERS, .....,** son of a laborer, was born in Duncarney in May 1769. His mother was aged 85. [SM.31.279]

**ROGERSON, JOHN,** Lord Chief Justice of King's Bench in Ireland, died 1741. [SM.3.382]

**Roscommon, Earl of,** died in Dublin on 21 August 1746. [SM.8.399]

**ROSE, JOHN,** an Alderman, died at Sandymount near Dublin on 30 May 1811. [SM.73.559]

**ROSE, .....,** a judge of the King's Bench in Ireland, died 1742. [SM.5.50]

**ROSE, ......,** son of Mr Rose of Pitcalnie, was born in Dublin on 14 October 1811. [SM.73.876]

**ROSS, DAVID ROBERT,** of Rostrevor, married Harriot Knox, second daughter of Reverend Dean of Down, and niece of Viscount Northland, in Dungannon on 21 October 1819. [SM.84.487]

**Ross, the Earl of,** an Irish peer, married Miss Edwards in Dublin on 16 February 1754. [SM.16.107]

**Ross, the Countess of Ross in Ireland,** died in London on 24 April 1768. [SM.30.223]

**ROSS, Captain,** of the 41$^{st}$ Regiment, married Miss Browne, daughter of the late Lord Kilmaine, and niece to the Earl of Charlemont, in Dublin on 30 April 1798. [SM.60.292]

**Ross, Earl RALPH of,** a representative peer of Ireland, died on 28 April 1807. 'He is succeeded by his nephew Sir Lawrence Parsons'. [SM.69.478]

**ROSS, .....,** daughter of Lieutenant Colonel Ross of the 23$^{rd}$ Light Dragoons, was born in Dublin on 29 August 1807. [SM.69.797]

**Rothes, the Countess of,** died in Dublin on 26 April 1761. [SM.23.223]

**ROWAN, G. WILLIAM HAMILTON,** Captain in the Royal Navy, son of A. Hamilton Rowan of Killileagh, County Down, married Catherine Cockburn, eldest daughter of Lieutenant General Cockburn of Rutland Square, and of Manganna, County Dublin, on 13 August 1817. [SM.80.193]

**ROWLEY, ELISABETH ORMSBY,** Viscountess Langford of Langford Lodge, County Antrim, died in Summerhill, County Meath, on 18 December 1791. [SM.53.622]

**ROWLEY, HERCULES LANGFORD,** died in Dublin on 25 March 1794. [SM.56.179]

**RUDD, Mrs,** 'the celebrated', died in Ireland, 1779. [SM.41.341]

**RUNDLE, Dr THOMAS,** Bishop of Derry, died at St Stephen's Green, Dublin, on 16 April 1743. [SM.5.197]

**RUTHERFORD, Captain ARCHIBALD,** of the 27th Foot, and son of the late Major Rutherford of Edgerston, died in Dublin on 16 August 1788. [SM.50.415]

**RYDER, Mr,** the celebrated comedian, died in Sandymount near Dublin on 26 December 1791. [SM.53.621]

**ST CLAIR, ........,** Captain of Forbes' Regiment of Foot, Secretary to the Earl of Rothes, died in Dublin on 12 February 1757. [SM.19.111]

**ST CLAIR, Captain WILLIAM STIRLING,** married Eliza Gordon, youngest daughter of the late Colonel Gordon of Feltrum, in County Fermanagh in 1808. [SM.71.77]

**ST FERROL, Lieutenant CHARLES,** aged 95, died in Dublin on 16 February 1758. 'he served in all King William's wars and lost an arm at the battle of the Boyne. [SM.20.110]

**ST GEORGE, ELIZABETH,** Baroness St George, of Hatley St George, grand-mother of the Duke of Leinster, died in Dublin on 26 February 1813, aged 81. [SM.75.318]

**ST GEORGE, ......,** son of Lady Harriet F. St George, was born in Tyrone in April 1810. [SM.72.477]

**ST GEORGE, ......,** son of Lady Harriet St George, was born in Tyrone on 15 July 1811. [SM.73.635]

**ST GEORGE, MANSERGH,** died in Ireland during 1790 of a wound received at the Battle of Germantown in America. [SM.52.464]

**ST GEORGE, Lieutenant General RICHARD,** Colonel of Dragoons, and a Major General on the Irish

Establishment, died in Dublin on 12 January 1755. [SM.17.52]

**ST GEORGE, RICHARD,** Member of Parliament for Charleville in Ireland, Inspector of Recruits in Ireland, Lieutenant Colonel of the 8$^{th}$ Regiment of Dragoons, died in Oporto, Portugal, on 10 April 1790. [SM.52.205]

**ST GEORGE, ROBERT,** married Miss Pringle, daughter of General Pringle, in Dublin in 1797. [SM.59.636]

**ST LAWRENCE, THOMAS,** Lord Lowth, an Irish peer, died in County Lowth, on 20 June 1754.[SM.16.308]

**ST LAWRENCE, Miss,** daughter of the Earl of Howth, married Lord Sydney, in Dublin in December 1773. [SM.35.670]

**ST LAWRENCE, Lord Viscount,** son of the Earl of Howth in Ireland, married Lady Mary Birmingham, daughter of the Earl of Louth, on 19 July 1777. [SM.39.390]

**ST LAWRENCE, Lord,** was flung from a high phaeton and killed near Dublin on 16 April 1779. [SM.41.221]

**ST LAWRENCE, the Viscountess,** second daughter of the Earl of Lowth, died in Ireland on 24 August 1793. [SM.55.413]

**ST LEGER, LOUIS ANNE,** sister of Viscount Doneraile, married Lieutenant Colonel Leighton of the Shropshire Militia, in London on 22 July 1805. [SM.67.726]

**ST LEGER, General,** died in Ireland in May 1786. [SM.48.259]

**ST LEGER, ......,** son of Lady Charlotte St Leger, was born in Doneraile House, Ireland, on 30 September 1818. [SM.82.484]

**SAMPSON, PATRICK,** aged 125, a gardener, died at Donore, County West Meath, on 10 March 1751. [SM.13.163]

**SANDFORD, Colonel,** married Lady Rachel McDonnel, sister to the Earl of Antrim, in Dublin in August 1777. [SM.39.453]

**SARLSFIELD, Reverend ,** aged 106, died in Cork on 7 November 1766. [SM.28.615]

**SAVAGE, FRANCIS,** Member of Parliament for County Down, married Miss Crawford, niece of John Crawford of Crawfordsburn, on 1 November 1795. [SM.57.748]

**Scarborourgh, the Earl of,** Vice Chancellor of Ireland, died on 12 May 1782. [SM.44.280]

**SCORY, ELIZABETH,** wife of Christopher Scory a laborer, gave birth to triplets in Dublin on 14 February 1752. [SM.14.156]

**SCOTT, JOHN,** Earl of Clonmell, Baron Earlsfort, Chief Justice of the Court of King's Bench, died in Dublin in 1798. [SM.60.507]

**SCOTT, .....,** son of Sir John Scott of Ancrum, was born in Athlone on 14 July 1798. [SM.60.507]

**SCULLY, ......,** a laborer in Glengarff near Bantry, father of quadruplets, three sons and a daughter born 1819. [SM.84.486]

**SEAVER, Mrs BRIDGET,** aged 108, relict of Jonathan Seaver, late of Treavey, County Armagh, died in Dublin during 1790. [SM.52.207]

**SHAIRP, Lieutenant Colonel GIDEON,** of the 9th Regiment of Foot, Deputy Quarter Master General, died in Armagh on 27 February 1806. [SM.67.318]

**Shannon, the Earl of,** Viscount Brandon, Lord Justice in Ireland, died aged 82. He was succeeded by his eldest son Viscount Boyle. [SM.27.55]

**Shannon, ....,** son of the Earl of Shannon, was born in Dublin on 6 February 1767, and died in March 1767. [SM.29.103/167]

**Shannon, .....,** son and heir of the Earl of Shannon, was born at Castle Martyr on 8 August 1771. [SM.33.445]

**Shannon, .....,** daughter of the Earl of Shannon was born on 29 September 1812. [SM.74.885]

**SHARP, Mr and Mrs,** 'died in Dublin within a few hours of each other. They were born on 1 April 1673, married on 1 April 1693, had their first daughter Maria on 1 April 1694, their first son on 1 April 1695, their second son on 2 April 1696, and their third son on 1 April 1696; they live in Londonderry. Maria was married at 18 on 1 April and had a son born on 1 April following James Witham Montgomery, now in a high post under the American Congress.' [SM.46.268]

**SHAW, Lieutenant Colonel HENRY,** of the 11th Foot, died in Cork in 1790. [SM.52.569]

**SHAW, SYLVIA,** youngest daughter of the late Robert Shaw in Dublin, married Pierre Felix Viennot, a

Chevalier of the Legion of Honor, on 16 January 1818.
[SM.81.193]

**SHEFFINGTON, HUNGERFORD,** uncle to the Earl of
Masserene, died in Antrim in September 1768.
[SM.30.559]

**SHERIDAN, RICHARD,** His Majesty's Counsel at Law
and Member of Parliament for Charlemont, died in
Dublin on 12 December 1793. [SM.55.621]

**SHERIDAN, ......,** Governor to the Young Pretender,
died in Rome in December 1746. [SM.8.598]

**SHERRARD, Lord,** Baron Leitrim in Ireland, died in
London on 24 February 1770. His brother Reverend
Sherrard succeeded to the lands and titles.
[SM.32.111]

**SHIELE, JAMES,** a farmer, aged 136, died at
Ballybooden near Knocktopher, County Kilkenny, on 1
April 1759. [SM.21.273]

**SHINNICK, Mrs MARY,** aged 104, died at Clerk's
Bridge, Cork, on 8 January 1821. [SM.87.191]

**SHONNEL, WILLIAM,** aged 102, a native of Ireland,
Captain of Los Rios Regiment of Infantry, died in
Brussels on 17 December 1753. [SM.15.581]

**SHORT, ......,** daughter of Charles Short of the 6th
Dragoon Guards, was born in the Royal Barracks in
Dublin on 2 February 1824. [SM.93.382]

**SHORTALL, THOMAS,** aged 104, born in Kilkenny,
died in Landreci, French Flanders, on 19 August 1762.
He was Captain of Grace's Regiment at the Siege of
Limerick in 1691, and afterwards, along with the
remains of the Irish army, went to France. He was
made a Knight of St Louis on 6 June 1729, and a

Lieutenant Colonel on 10 June 1745 after the Battle of Fontenoy. [SM.24.567]

**SHULDHAM, LEMUEL,** brother of Admiral Lord Shuldham, died in Kilkenny in August 1776. [SM.38.455]

**SIMPSON, WILLIAM,** aged 119, a farmer, died in Laymore near Ballymena in December 1804. [SM.67.77]

**SINGLETON, HENRY,** Master of the Rolls and late Lord Chief Justice of Common Pleas in Ireland, died in Dublin on 9 November 1759. [SM.21.607]

**SKEFFINGTON, CLOTWORTHY,** Earl of Massareene, died at his seat in County Antrim on 14 September 1757. [SM.19.495]

**Sligo, ......,** daughter of the Marquis of Sligo, was born in 1816. [SM.79.158]

**Sligo, ......,** daughter of the Marquis of Sligo, was born in Westport House on 2 December 1817. [SM.81.94]

**Sligo, the Dowager Marchioness of,** born 9 December 1767, died in Amsterdam on 26 August 1817. [SM.80.195]

**Sligo, ......,** son of the Marquis of Sligo, was born on 31 January 1820. [SM.85.290]

**SLOANE, Sir HANS,** born in Killelagh, County Down, physician to the King, died in Chelsea on 11 January 1753. [SM.15.52]

**SLOANE, JOHN,** aged 101, died in Scrabby, County Cavan, on 22 August 1758. 'He served at the Siege of Londonderry and as a Lieutenant of Horse under King William'. [SM.20.443]

**SLOPER, Captain,** son of General Sloper, and one of the ADCs to the late Lord Lieutenant of Ireland, died in 1787. [SM.49.570]

**SMART, HENRY,** a musical professor and brother of Sir George Smart MD, died in Dublin on 14 November 1823. [SM.93.127]

**SMITH, GEORGE,** a Baron of the Exchequer in Ireland, died in Bath on 16 February 1772. [SM.34.111]

**SMITH, JANE,** a fisherman's wife in Kinsale, was delivered of four sons on 22 October 1750. [SM.12.550]

**SMITH, JOHN,** a Lieutenant in the Royal Navy, married Miss McDowall, daughter of Francis McDowell, in Sligo in 1798. [SM.61.71]

**SMITH, Alderman,** Lord Mayor elect of Dublin for 1793, died there on 17 September 1792. [SM.53.467]

**SMITH, ......,** Colonel of the 3$^{rd}$ Garrison Battalion, died in Bray in 1809. [SM.71.880]

**SMYTH, OSWALD,** died in Londonderry in May 1807. [SM.69.479]

**SMYTH, Major General,** Colonel of the 63$^{rd}$ Regiment of Foot, died in Dublin on 1 November 1768. [SM.30.613]

**SMYTH, ......,** son of Lady Isabella Smyth, was born in Dublin on 12 September 1818. [SM.82.389]

**SOUTHWELL, JAMES,** aged 106, died in Limerick on 10 November 1782. 'He fought under the Duke of Marlborough at the battle of Malplaquet in 1708 ..seven of his brothers were killed that day....he lived in Limerick for over 60 years as a day laborer.... he buried 7 wives and was married to his eighth, he had 37 children, 83 grandchildren, 25 great grandchildren, and 11 great great grandchildren, in all 156'. [SM.44.615]

**SOUTHWELL, ROBERT HENRY,** late of Castle Hamilton, County Cavan, formerly Lieutenant Colonel of the 8th Dragoons, died at Clontarff near Dublin on 29 August 1817. [SM.80.195]

**Southwell, THOMAS, Lord,** born 7 January 1698, of the kingdom of Ireland, a Privy Councillor, died in London on 19 November 1766. [SM.28.615]

**SPEAR, Lieutenant WILLIAM,** aged 81, died in Spearvale, County Cavan, on 18 May 1819. [SM.83.95]

**SPENCER, PAUL,** a traveller through Europe, Asia and Africa, died at Muff, County Londonderry, on 11 September 1767. [SM.29.501]

**SPOTTISWOOD, Mrs AGNES,** relict of Robert Duncan, died in Lisburn on 26 September 1807. [SM.69.876]

**STAFFORD, BERKELEY BUCKINGHAM SMITH,** of Maine, County Louth, married Ann Tytler, daughter of Lieutenant Commander Patrick Tytler, on 3 July 1818. [SM.82.103]

**STAPLES, JOHN,** aged 85, a Privy Councillor, died in Lissau, Ireland, on 30 December 1820. [SM.87.191]

**STAPLES, Mrs,** eldest daughter of Sir James Stewart of Fort Stewart, County Donegal, married Richard Napier, son of the late Colonel Napier, at Bath on 1 September 1817. [SM.80.193]

**Stavordale, Lord,** eldest son of the Earl of Ilchester, married Mary Grady, daughter of Standish Grady, in

Cappercullen, County Limerick, on 3 September 1772. [SM.34.516]

**STEELE, WALTER,** of Monalry, County Monaghan, married Maria Sophia Jocelyn, fourth daughter of the late George Jocelyn and niece of the Earl of Roden, in Dublin on 28 July 1818. [SM.82.199]

**STEIN, JOHN,** married Miss Colclough, only daughter of Charles Colclough, in Dublin in 1811. [SM.73.637]

**STERNE, Dr JOHN,** aged 85, Bishop of Clogher, died there on 6 June 1745. [SM.7.297]

**STEUART, Colonel JOHN,** died in Dublin on 24 October 1762. 'He was the survivor of four brothers, William, Charles, John, and James, sons of Colonel John Steuart and nephews of the late Lieutenant General William Steuart of Hanover Square, London. They were descended from the Earls of Galloway in Scotland and bear the same arms; and have left behind three sons; William, the only son of Charles, settled in the County of Cavan in Ireland; William, the only son of John, settled in the County of Carlow, in the same kingdom; and James, the only son of James Steuart [the youngest of the four brothers and late Admiral of the fleet, who is now, or lately was, at Paddington school. The other brother, William, the eldest of them, a brigadier general in the service of Queen Anne, died long since, without issue, at Bath, where a monument is erected for him in the Abbey church.' [SM.24.623]

**STEUART, Captain,** of the Royal Irish Dragoons, son of Sir James Steuart of Coltness, married Alice Blacker, daughter of John Blacker of Carrick, in Ireland on 30 September 1772. [SM.34.582]

**STEVENSON, DAVID,** born in Mauchline, Ayrshire, a merchant in Limerick, died at his house in Cecil Street, Limerick, in 1821. [SM.88.296]

**STEWART, ALEXANDER ROBERT,** MP for County Londonderry, eldest son of Alexander Stewart of Ards in County Donegal, married Lady Caroline Ann Pratt, youngest daughter of the Marquis and Marchioness Camden, at St George's church, Hanover Square, London, on 28 July 1825. [SM.96.382]

**STEWART, ANDREW THOMAS,** Earl of Castle Stewart, died 'at a very advanced age' at Stewart Hall, County Tyrone, on 26 August 1809. 'He was the acknowledged head of the House of Stewart being immediately descended, in the male and legitimate line, from Robert II, King of Scotland. [SM.71.719]

**STEWART, Lady EMILY JANE,** daughter of the Earl of Londonderry, and sister to Viscount Castlereagh, and Lieutenant General Lord Stewart a Knight of the Bath, married John James, son of Walter James James of Langley Hall, Berkshire, Secretary of Legation at the Court of Munich, at Mount Stewart on 28 June 1814. [SM.76.638]

**STEWART, HENRY,** Member of Parliament for Longford, married Miss Pakenham, eldest daughter of the late Lord Longford, at Summer Hill, Ireland, the seat of Mr Rowley, in 1793. [SM.55.100]

**STEWART, JOHN,** of Stewartfield, Lieutenant Colonel of Wynyard's Regiment of Foot, died in Ireland on 2 February 1750. [SM.12.102]

**STEWART, ROBERT,** married Lady Sarah Conway, second daughter of the Earl of Hertford, Lord

Lieutenant of Ireland, in Dublin on 3 June 1764. [SM.28.335]

**STEWART, Lady SARAH,** wife of Robert Stewart, and daughter of the Earl of Hertford, died in Dublin on 18 July 1770. [SM.32.398]

**STEWART, WILLIAM,** Earl of Blessington in Ireland, died in London on 14 August 1769. [SM.31.447]

**STEWART, ......,** daughter of Lady Mary Stewart, was born in Londonderry on 19 September 1792. [SM.53.518]

**STEWART, Lieutenant Colonel,** of the 80th Regiment, married Miss Hyde, eldest daughter of John Hyde of Creeg, in Cork in 1802. [SM.64.615]

**STEWART, Captain,** third brother of Lord Castlereagh, born 27 August 1790, died in Portugal in 1810. [SM.72.799]

**STEWART, ......,** son of James Stewart, was born in Clontarff near Dublin on 27 May 1822. [SM.92.127]

**STIRLING, ROBERT,** Captain of the Royal Regiment of Foot of Ireland, died in Dublin on 3 March 1754. [SM.16.154]

**STOCK, JOSEPH,** Bishop of Waterford, aged 77, died there on 13 August 1813. [SM.75.719]

**STODDART, Major JOHN,** of the 45th Regiment of Foot, died in Ballyshannon on 2 January 1814. [SM.76.237]

**STODDART, Lieutenant THOMAS,** of the 2nd Regiment of Irish Light Dragoons, married Jane Catherine Ralston, daughter of Gavin Ralston of Ralston, in Cork on 4 January 1798. [SM.60.72]

**STONE, Dr GEORGE,** Archbishop of Armagh and Primate of All Ireland, died in London on 19 December 1764. [SM.26.687]

**STONE, Mrs,** sister of the late Lord Primate, was killed in Ireland on 9 March 1769 by the breaking down of a coach. [SM.31.166]

**STOPFORD, Dr JAMES,** Bishop of Cloyne, died in Dublin on 23 August 1759. [SM.21.445]

**Stopford, Lord,** eldest son of the Earl of Castletown in Ireland, married Miss Powis, in London on 19 April 1762. [SM.24.226]

**STOPFORD, Reverend Dr,** Bishop of Cork and Ross, died at his palace near Cork on 15 January 1805. [SM.67.159]

**STORY, Dr JOSEPH,** Bishop of Kilmore, died at Kilmore, Ireland, on 18 September 1757. [SM.19.495]

**Strangford, .....,** son of Lord Viscount Strangford, was born in Londonderry on 19 May 1753. [SM.15.261]

**Strangford, Lord Viscount,** died in Palmerstown, Ireland, in May 1787. [SM.49.259]

**Strangford, .......,** son of Lady Strangford, was born in Constantinople on 5 August 1821. [SM.88.392]

**STUART, GEORGE,** Captain of the 3$^{rd}$ [Buffs] Regiment, married Alicia Inston Dunkin, only daughter of the late Reverend Henry Dunkin rector of Glasslough, County Monaghan, on 1 November 1818. [SM.82.587]

**STUART, HUGH,** uncle to Lord Blantyre, died in Ireland in February 1769. [SM.31.110]

**STUART, Major General JAMES,** died at Black Rock near Dublin in 1798. [SM.60.363]

**STUART, Captain JOHN,** commander of HMS Saldana, second son of the late General Sir Charles Stuart, Knight of the Bath, and nephew to the Marquis of Bute, and the Lord Primate of Ireland, died in Lough Swilly on 19 March 1811. [SM.73.320]

**STUART, WILLIAM,** MP, eldest son of the Lord Primate of Ireland, married Henrietta Pole, eldest daughter of Admiral Sir C. Pole, in St Mary-la-Bonne Church, London, on 9 August 1821. [SM.88.293]

**STUART, .......,** son and heir of A. Stuart, was born in Belmount, Tyrone, on 30 December 1814. [SM.77.159]

**STUPART, FRANCIS,** Captain of the Royal North British Dragoons [the Scots Greys], married Anne Jameson daughter of John Jameson in Alloa, in Dublin on 9 April 1821. [SM.87.494]

**SUDLEY, Lord Viscount,** son of the Earl of Aran in Ireland, married Miss Tyrell, eldest daughter of the late Sir John Tyrell of Heron, Essex, on 29 December 1787. [SM.49.620]

**SUTHERLAND, GEORGE SINCLAIR,** a Lieutenant of the Ross-shire and Caithness Fencibles, died in Dublin in 1794. [SM.56.735]

**SWAN, Reverend BELLINGHAM,** aged 102, died in Desart, Ireland, in 1798. 'He was curate to Dean Swift'. [SM.60.729]

**SWAN, DAVID,** late merchant in Leith, died in Dublin in 1812. [SM.74.318]

**SWAN, EDWARD BELLINGHAM,** MP, Commissioner for the Imprest Office and for Stamp Duties, died in Dublin on 21 September 1788. [SM.50.467]

**SWEATMAN, the Right Reverend Dr NICHOLAS,** the Bishop of Wexford for 42 years, died there on 21 October 1786. [SM.48.569]

**SWIFT, Dr JONATHAN,** aged 78, Dean of St Patrick's in Dublin, died there on 19 October 1745. [SM.7.494]

**Sydney, Lord, of Leix,** Baron of Stradbally, died in Stradbally, Queen's County, Ireland, on 26 January 1774. [SM.36.55]

**SYNGE, Dr EDWARD,** Lord Archbishop of Tuam, Primate of Connaught, died in Tuam, 23 July 1741. [SM.3.331]

**SYNGE, Dr EDWARD,** Bishop of Elphin, died in Dublin on 29 January 1762. [SM.24.56]

**SYNGE, Dr NICHOLAS,** Archbishop of Killaloe, died in Ireland on 26 January 1771. [SM.33.54]

**TALBOT, Lady FRANCES CHARLOTTE CHETWYND,** eldest daughter of Earl Talbot, Lord Lieutenant of Ireland, married the Earl of Dartmouth, in Cirencester, on 5 April 1821. [SM.87.494]

**TALBOT, Colonel,** of Malahide in Ireland, died in 1788. [SM.50.570]

**Talbot, .....,** son of the Countess of Talbot, was born in Dublin on 3 October 1819. [SM.84.485]

**Talbot, the Countess of,** died at Vice Regal Lodge, Dublin, on 30 December 1819. [SM.85.190]

**TANDY, EDWARD,** a Major in the service of the East India Company, died in Bullingate, County Wicklow, on 24 August 1819. [SM.84.359]

**TAYLOR, JOHN,** of Blackhouse, Ayrshire, married Mary Taylor, second daughter of Captain Taylor of Camden Street, Dublin, in Dublin on 10 July 1812. [SM.74.645]

**TEMPLETOWN, Lord,** of County Antrim, married Miss Rietz, a natural daughter of the King of Prussia, in 1793. 'Her mother, Mrs Rietz, was for many years the favourite mistress of the King of Prussia'. [SM.55.152]

**THOM, WALTER,** from Aberdeen, former editor of *'The Correspondent'* and lately joint proprietor and editor of the *'Dublin Journal'*, died in Dublin on 16 June 1824. [SM.94.255]

**THOMAS, DANIEL,** aged 108, a laborer, died in Glanmire near Cork in 1787. [SM.49.518]

**THOMAS, DAVID,** of the 92$^{nd}$ [Gordon Highlanders], married Miss Caldos, daughter of Captain Caldos of the Donegal Militia, in Downpatrick on 16 November 1817. [SM.80.498]

**Thomond, MURROUGH, Marquis of,** aged 85, husband of Miss Palmer niece of Sir Joshua Reynolds, died in London, 10 February 1808. His title, Marquis of Thomond, and estates descended to his nephew Captain O'Brian. [SM.70.238]

**THOMSON, JAMES,** Major of the Royal Scots, died at Dundalk, Ireland, on 10 June 1754. [SM.16.308]

**THOMPSON, JAMES,** aged 104, died in Mecklenburg Street, Dublin, on 9 May 1769. [SM.31.279]

**THOMPSON, JOHN,** eldest son of Ross Thompson of Lawrencetown, County Down, married Helen Robertson, youngest daughter of John Robertson of the Crescent, Bath, there on 15 April 1808. [SM.71.397]

**TICKEL, THOMAS,** secretary to the Lords Justices of Ireland, died 1740. [SM.2.1740]

**TILSON, ELIZABETH ANN,** Lady Castlecoote, eldest daughter of Henry Tilson, DD, of Eagle Hill, County Kildare, died 18 January 1821. [SM.87.192]

**Tingall, ......,** son of the Earl of Tingall in Ireland, was born in Woolhampron, Berkshire, on 9 September 1759. [SM.21.500]

**TIPPING, Miss,** daughter of Thomas Tipping of Beaulieu, County Lowth, MP for Kilbeggan, married Cadwallander, Lord Blaney, in Ireland in December 1767. [SM.29.669]

**TISDALL, Mrs ANNE,** aged 110, died in Dublin on 18 September 1757. 'She was born in Coventry and went to Ireland in Cromwell's time'. [SM.19.495]

**TOMLIN, MARY, ELIZABETH, and ANNE,** daughters of a poultryman in Dublin, were born on 16 August 1753. [SM.15.422]

**TONNERY, HENRY,** aged 112, an apothecary, died in Waterford in 1791. [SM.53.362]

**TOOLE, BRIDGET,** aged 103, died in Plunket Street, Dublin, on 16 January 1769. [SM.31.54]

**TOUCHET, JAMES,** Earl of Castlehaven in Ireland, died in Paris, 1740. [SM.2.535]

**TOUCHET, JAMES,** Earl of Castlehaven in Ireland, died in Wiltshire on 8 May 1769. [SM.31.279]

**TOUCHET, JOHN TALBOT,** Earl of Castlehaven in Ireland, died in Bath on 22 April 1777. [SM.39.223]

**Townshend, FREDERICK,** son of the Lord Lieutenant of Ireland, was born in Dublin Castle on 30 December 1767. [SM.30.54]

**TOWNSHEND, PATRICK CHARLES,** son of Viscount Townshend, was born in Leixslip Castle near Dublin on 6 January 1769. He was baptised by the Archbishop of Dublin at Leixslip, the sponsors were Lord Annaly the Lord Chief Justice of King's Bench, the Hon. Thomas Conolly, and Lady Elisabeth Southwell, on 7 February 1769 [SM.31.54/110]

**Townshend, Viscountess,** died in Dublin on 5 September 1770. [SM.32.558]

**TOWNSHEND, Lieutenant Colonel,** of the 75th Regiment of Foot, died in Ireland in March 1773. [SM.35.165]

**TOWNSLEY, GEORGE, FREDERICK, and FERDINAND,** sons of Andrew Townsley, a private soldier in General Handisyd's regiment, were born in Dublin on 14 April 1762. [SM.24.227]

**TRACTON, Baron,** Chief Baron of the Court of the Exchequer in Ireland, and one of the Lords of the Privy Council of Ireland, died in Ireland on 8 June 1782. [SM.44.334]

**TRACY, Reverend Lord Viscount JOHN,** aged 71, DD, Viscount and Baron Tracy of Rathcoole, County Dublin, Warden of All Souls College, died in Bath on 2 February 1793. [SM.55.101]

**TRACY, THOMAS CHARLES,** eldest son of Lord Viscount Tracy an Irish peer, married Harriot Bathurst, daughter of Lady Selina Bathurst, at Lidney Park on 6 February 1755. [SM.17.108]

**TRAIL, CATHERINE,** only daughter of Reverend Archdeacon Trail, died in Lisburn on 23 March 1823. [SM.91.648]

**TRAIL, JAMES,** Under Secretary to the Lord Lieutenant of Ireland, died in Dublin, 1808. [SM.70.719]

**TRAIL, Reverend Dr,** of Lisburn, married Lady Frances Charteris, daughter of the Earl of Wemyss, in Edinburgh on 29 April 1799. [SM.61.283]

**TRAIL, Mrs,** mother of the present Bishop of Down, died in Dundee on 15 September 1766. [SM.28.503]

**TRANT, DOMINICK,** brother in law to the Lord Chancellor of Ireland, King's Advocate of the Court of the Admiralty of Ireland, and late chairman of the Quarter Sessions of County Tipperary, died in Cahir, County Tipperary, in 1790. 'This gentleman had the misfortune to kill Sir John Colthurst in a duel.' [SM.52.363]

**TREFFY, LOUGHLIN,** aged 110, a mason, died near Gort in County Galway in August 1767. [SM.29.501]

**TRENCH, Lieutenant General EYRE POWER,** brother of the late Earl of Clancarty, died in Kilkenny on 20 July 1808. [SM.70.560]

**TREVOR, ARTHUR,** only son of Lord Viscount Dungannon, and a representative in parliament for Hillsborough, died in Dublin on 18 June 1770. [SM.32.343]

**TREVOR, ARTHUR,** Viscount Duncannon, died in Ireland on 26 January 1771. [SM.33.109]

**Trindlestown, Lord,** married Alicia Eustace, daughter of Major General Eustace, in Dublin in 1797. [SM.59.636]

**TROTTER, ......,** son of Mary Trotter, was born in Springfield near Dublin on 11 September 1807. [SM.69.798]

**TROTTER, THOMAS,** Judge of the Prerogative and Consistory Courts, a Member of Parliament, etc., died in Dublin on 25 October 1745. [SM.7.542]

**TROTTER, Major General THOMAS,** Commandant of the Royal Artillery in Ireland, died in Dublin on 6 March 1819. [SM.83.385]

**TROTTER, Lieutenant Colonel,** of the 113rd Regiment, died in Dublin on 29 December 1795. [SM.57.818]

**TROY, WILLIAM,** aged 120, died near Waterford in 1792. [SM.53.519]

**TROY, Dr,** aged 83, Roman Catholic Archbishop of Dublin, died there on 10 May 1823. [SM.91.776]

**TRUMBLE, Reverend MATTHEW,** for 40 years the minister of the Presbyterian congregation in Monaghan, died there on 7 March 1821. [SM.87.400]

**TURNERO, .....,** quadruplets of ... Turnero a gauger, were born in Longford Pass near Dublin in June 1755. [SM.17.316]

**TWYSDEN, Dr PHILIP,** Bishop of Raphoe, died in London on 2 November 1752. [SM.14.510]

**TYLER, HENRY HUBY,** of Newton Limnavady, married Helen McLarty of Greenock, there on 4 April 1808. [SM.70.316]

**Tylney, JOHN, Earl of,** died in Naples, where he had resided for many years, on 17 September 1784. [SM.46.554]

**Tyrawley, JAMES, Lord Baron,** aged 74, died at Castlelacken, County Mayo, on 15 June 1821. [SM.88.95]

**Tyrconnel, GEORGE, Earl of,** died in London on 9 March 1762. [SM.24.167]

**Tyrconnel, the Earl of,** married Lady Frances Manners, daughter of the late Marquis of Granby, in Chiswick on 9 July 1772. [SM.34.398]

**Tyrone, ......,** son of the Earl of Tyrone, was born in Ireland on 18 May 1772. [SM.34.276]

**Tyrone, GEORGE, Earl of,** eldest son of the Marquis of Waterford, died on 8 July 1824. [SM.94.256]

**Upper Ossory,........,** son of the Earl of Upper Ossory, was born in London on 5 May 1755. [SM.17.268]

**URQUHART, WILLLIAM,** a Captain of the Royal Essex Fencibles, died at Ballyshannon in September 1798. [SM.60.720]

**USHER, Reverend H.,** D.D., senior Fellow of Trinity College, and St Andrew's Professor of Astronomy in the university, and member of the Royal Academy, died in Dublin on 8 May 1790. [SM.52.258]

**USHER, Miss,** daughter of Archibald Usher, married Richard, Lord Viscount Molesworth, a Lieutenant General, in Dublin on 8 February 1744. [SM.6.98]

**VANCE, GEORGE,** aged 119, died in the parish of Clonsecle, County Tyrone, on 3 January 1758. 'he had a full set of new teeth four years before'. [SM.20.51]

**VANDELEUR, JOHN ORMSBY,** aged 55, from County Limerick, late an army colonel and Lieutenant Colonel of the 5th Dragoon Guards, died at Clifton, Bristol, on 3 November 1822. [SM.89.752]

**VAUGHAN, JOHN,** Lord Viscount Lisburne in Ireland, died at Crosswood, Cardiganshire, 1740. [SM.3.47]

**VAUGHAN, Captain,** son and heir apparent of Lord Viscount Lilbourne of Ireland, married Miss Nightingale, only daughter of Joseph Gascoigne Nightingale, late of Enfield, in July 1754. [SM.16.356]

**Ventry, Lord,** died in Burnham House, County Kerry, on 11 January 1824. [SM.93.256]

**VESEY, Sir JOHN DENNY,** Lord Baron Knapton, died at his seat near Merrion on 26 June 1761. 'He is succeeded by his only son Thomas, a Lieutenant in the Earl of Drogheda's regiment.' [SM.23.336]

**VILLIERS, JOHN FITZGERALD,** aged 85, Earl and Viscount Grandison of Limerick, uncle to Mr Pitt, husband of Frances, daughter of Anthony Carey, Lord Viscount Falkland, Premier Viscount of Scotland, died in Dublin on 7 May 1766. [SM.28.336]

**WAINWRIGHT, JOHN,** third Baron of the Exchequer in Ireland, died 1741. [SM.3.191]

**WALCOTT, Captain THOMAS,** late of the 12th Regiment of Foot, third son of John Minchin Walcott of Creagh, County Limerick, died in Inverness in 1815. [SM.77.400]

**WALKER, THOMAS,** of the Scots Greys, married Constantia Frances Anne Beresford, eldest daughter of J.C.Beresford, in Dalteath, County Londonderry, on 21 April 1819. [SM.83.583]

**WALL, .....,** son of Major Wall of the 35$^{th}$ Regiment, was born in Wexford on 23 July 1820. [SM.86.285]

**WALLACE, JOHN,** 'one of the oldest barristers at the Irish bar', died in Dublin on 29 September 1806. [SM.67.808]

**WALLACE, ROBERT,** married Catherine Matilda Templeton, daughter of the late Thomas Templeton of Calcutta, in Newry on 27 August 1819. [SM.84.293]

**WALLACE, ........,** son of Major Wallace of the King's Dragoon Guards, was born in Dundalk on 9 March 1820. [SM.85.388]

**WALLIS, Miss,** eldest daughter of the late Hector Wallis formerly of Springmount, Queen's County, married Lord Mountjoy, at Golden Grove, King's County, in 1793. [SM.55.567]

**WALSH, Dr PHILIP,** aged 26, born in Kilkenny, a physician and lecturer in midwifery, died in London on 26 December 1787. [SM.49.623]

**WALSH, Dr RICHARD,** titular Bishop of Cork, died there on 6 January 1763. [SM.25.59]

**WALSH, VALENTINE,** aged 109, a farmer, died at Glencullen near Kilternan, County Dublin, on 4 June 1808. [SM.70.557]

**WALSINGHAM, CHARLES BOYLE,** a cornet in Conway's Horse, second son and aide-de-camp to the Earl of Shannon, Lord Justice of Ireland, died at Hot Wells, Bristol, on 30 May 1758. [SM.20.331]

**WARD, EDWARD,** eldest son of Robert Ward , Colonel of the South Down Regiment of Militia, married Lady Matilda Stewart, daughter of the Earl of Londonderry, in County Down on 14 September 1815. [SM.77.873]

**WARD, MICHAEL,** a Justice of the King's Bench in Ireland, died at his seat at Castle Ward, County Down, on 21 February 1759. [SM.21.158]

**WARD, RALPH,** surveyor general and controller of the Ordnance Office in Ireland, died 6 September 1788. [SM.50.467]

**WARD, SAMUEL,** of Dublin, died in Edinburgh on 5 December 1808. [SM.70.960]

**WARD, SAMUEL,** only son of the late Samuel Ward of Dublin, died on 25 March 1812. [SM.74.319]

**WARDLAW, Colonel,** of the 76th Regiment, married Anne Lake, youngest daughter of the late Lord Viscount Lake, in Dublin on 6 July 1812. [SM.74.645]

**WARREN, Captain JAMES,** died at Grange, County Kilkenny, on 24 December 1757. He served under the Duke of Marlborough, and was at the battles of Hochslet, Malplaquet, and at the sieges of Lisle, Douai, and Ghent, and at the battle of Sheriffmuir. [SM.20.51]

**WARREN, JONAS,** aged 107, died near Baldoyle, Ireland, on 1 June 1787. For 95 years he was a fisherman. [SM.49.311]

**WARREN, Sir PETER,** Knight of the Bath, Vice Admiral of the White, MP, died in Dublin in July 1752. [SM.14.366]

**WARREN, Sir R.,** baronet, aged 87, died in Cork in 1811. [SM.73.960]

**WARREN, Mrs,** of Tollagh, County Dublin, aged 112, died in Dublin in 1794

**Waterford, ........,** son and heir of the Marquis of Waterford, was born in Tyrone House, Dublin, on 29 January 1810. [SM.72.237]

**Waterford, ........,** daughter of the Marquis of Waterford, was born in Dublin on 19 June 1815. [SM.77.638]

**WEBB, Lieutenant General,** Colonel of the 14th Regiment o Dragoons, died in Dublin on 9 November 1773. [SM.35.416]

**WEBSTER, CHARLES WEDDERBURN,** of the Carabiniers, married Rebecca Chatterton, youngest daughter of the late Sir James Chatterton of Castle Mahon, County Cork, in Douglas Church near Cork on 11 December 1822. [SM.91.127]

**WELCH, .....,** aged 11, twin sons of a butcher, died at Glamitskale, County Galway, in May 1755. [SM.17.268]

**WELSH, MARY,** wife of John Anderson a merchant in Dumfries, and daughter of William Welsh of Collin, died in Cork on 16 December 1788. [SM.51.49]

**WELSH, Mrs,** aged 102, relict of Reverend Mr Welsh of Blessington, died in Coleraine on 31 July 1769. 'she left numerous offspring to the amount of 102'. [SM.31.447]

**WEMYSS, Mrs,** wife of Major Wemyss, died in Dublin on 12 October 1790. [SM.52.518]

**WENMAN, Sir PHILIP,** Lord Viscount Wenman of Tuam, aged 41, MP for Oxford, died at Thame Park, Oxfordshire, on 16 August 1760. [SM.22.447]

**WESLEY, RICHARD,** Lord Mornington, an Irish peer, died in Dublin on 31 January 1758. He was succeeded by his only son Garret Wesley. [SM.20.52]

**WEST, WILLIAM,** aged over 90, died at Clouncarrig, County Kerry, on 11 March 1752. 'He left 110 children, grand-children, and great-grandchildren, most of whom attended the funeral'. [SM.14.156]

**Westmeath, the Earl of,** married Katherine Whyte, daughter of the late Henry Whyte in Pitchford's town, Kildare, on 7 August 1756. [SM.18.416]

**Westmeath, .......,** son of the Earl of Westmeath, was born in Ireland on 25 March 1759. [SM.21.217]

**Westmeath, .......,** son of the Earl of Westmeath, was born in Dublin on 24 November 1762. [SM.24.678]

**Westmeath, ......,** daughter of the Earl of Westmeath, was born in Ireland on 6 April 1766. [SM.28.222]

**Westmeath, the Countess of,** died in Dublin on 3 August 1772. [SM.34.453]

**Westmeath, the Earl of,** married Lady Elizabeth Moore, daughter of the Marquis of Drogheda in 1797. [SM.59.214]

**Westmeath, the Earl of,** died in Dublin on 30 December 1814. [SM.77.80]

**Westmoreland, ......,** daughter of the Earl of Westmoreland, was born in Dublin on 25 August 1793. [SM.55.412]

**Westmoreland, the Countess of,** died in Dublin Castle on 11 November 1793. [SM.55.570]

**WHELAN, JAMES,** aged 108, died at Birr on 29 July 1755. 'He has left 72 children and grand-children'. [SM.17.460]

**WHETCOMBE, Dr JOHN,** Archbishop of Cashel, aged 60, died in Ireland on 22 September 1753. [SM.15.525]

**WHITE, EDMUND,** aged 105, a farmer at Ballycuarragh near Lougrea, died in March 1768. [SM.30.223]

**WHITE, JOHN,** eldest son of the late John White of Esk Mills, died in Athlone on 20 November 1825. [SM.97.255]

**WHITE, KATHARINE,** aged 116, died at Shercock, County Cavan, on 11 April 1755. [SM.17.210]

**WHITE, LUKE,** MP for County Leitrim, died in London in 1824. [SM.93.646]

**WHITEFORD, Colonel CHARLES,** died in Galway on 24 December 1752. [SM.15.52]

**WHITSHED, Brigadier SAMUEL WALTER,** aged 60, died in Dublin on 14 March 1746. [SM.8.150]

**Wicklow, ROBERT, Earl of, Baron Clonmore,** died in Dublin on 23 October 1815. [SM.77.959]

**Wicklow, WILLIAM, Earl of,** died in Dublin on 27 September 1818. [SM.82.392]

**WILEY, NATHANIEL,** aged 106, died at Clogh near Ballymena on 19 February 1758. 'He was petty constable of Ballymena when King James XII's army marched in 1689 to besiege Londonderry. He used to say, he served two kings in one day; King William in the forenoon, out of love; and King James in the afternoon out of fear'. [SM.20.110]

**WILKINS, THOMAS,** aged 102, M.D., surgeon of the Galway County Infirmary, died in Galway in 1814. 'It was in to his arms the immortal Wolfe breathed his last after Quebec had surrendered to His Majesty's forces on 18 October 1759'. [SM.76.400]

**WILLIAMS, ......,** son of Colonel Sir William Williams of the 13th Regiment of Foot, was born in Londonderry on 28 April 1823. [SM.91.774]

**WILLIAMSON, J.,** Ensign of the 45th Regiment of Foot, second son of Joseph Williamson principal Clerk of Teinds, died in Ballyshannon on 21 April 1805. [SM.67.565]

**WILLIAMSON, JOSEPH,** Principal Clerk of Teinds, married Sarah Dove, relict of Robert Sinclair Lynd, late surgeon in the Royal Navy, in Kilmore near Dublin on 15 October 1805. [SM.67.804]

**WILLIAMSON, Lieutenant Colonel,** of the 39th Regiment of Foot, died in Dublin on 9 December 1767. [SM.29.610]

**WILSON, JOHN,** Secretary to the General Post Office in Dublin, died on 20 April 1771. [SM.33.221]

**WILSON, Reverend JOSIAS,** of Drogheda, married Mary Carlisle, daughter of James Carlisle, in Paisley on 25 December 1823. [SM.93.255]

**WILSON, WALTER,** late of Croglin, Dumfries-shire, died in Maryville near Belfast on 12 April 1807. [SM.69.320]

**WILSON, Mrs .....,** in Cunagstown, County Meath, aged 90, died 20 July 1753, mother of nine children. [SM.15.422]

**WIMS, THOMAS,** aged 117, died in the suburbs of Tuam in 1791. 'He fought in 1691 at the Siege of Londonderry, and in different skirmishes in the last and present century'. [SM.53.49]

**WINGFIELD, Reverend EDWARD,** second son of the late Lord Viscount Powerscourt, married Louisa Joan Jocelyn, daughter of the late George Jocelyn and niece of the Earl of Roden, in Dublin on 12 April 1819. [SM.83.479]

**WOOD, Lieutenant,** of the Fifeshire Fencibles, died in Londonderry on 11 January 1795. [SM.58.72]

**WOODS, ALEXANDER,** of Mountshannon, County Galway, died in Dublin on 24 January 1766. 'he was the first introducer of the linen manufacturer into that part of the kingdom'. [SM.28.55]

**WOODS, JOHN,** aged 122, a farmer, died at Gortnagally near Dungannon on 4 May 1818. 'His wife died about two years ago aged 82'. [SM.81.598]

**WOODS, JOSEPH,** aged 112, died in County Down on 3 April 1777. [SM.39.223]

**WOODWORTH, JOHN,** aged 112, died in Queen's County, in September 1780. [SM.42.617]

**WYNDHAM, THOMAS,** Lord Baron Wyndham of Finglas in Ireland, for several years Lord Chancellor of Ireland, died in London on 24 November 1745. [SM.7.543]

**WYNNE. JOHN,** Lieutenant Colonel of Molesworth's Dragoons, died in Sligo 1747. [SM.9.98]

**WYNNE, OWEN,** Member of Parliament for Sligo, married Sarah Cole, eldest daughter of the Earl of Enniskillen, at Florence Court in Ireland in 1789. [SM.52.49]

**WYSE, T.,** of the Manor of St John near Waterford, married Leitia Bonaparte, daughter of Lucien Bonaparte, Prince of Canino, and brother of the former Emperor of France, at the Palace of Canino near Rome on 4 April 1821. [SM.87.494]

**WYVIL, Sir MARMADUKE,** Post Master General of Ireland, died in Dublin on 28 December 1753. [SM.15.628]

**YOUNG, Dr EDWARD,** Bishop of Leighlin and Ferns, died in Ireland on 29 September 1772. [SM.34.517]

**YOUNG, Reverend ROBERT,** a clergyman of the Church of Ireland, and chaplain to the 21st Regiment of Ireland, and the Royal North British Fusiliers, died in Tralee on 21 May 1787. [SM.49.361]

**YOUNG, Reverend Dr.,** Roman Catholic Bishop of Limerick, died in Park near Limerick on 24 August 1813. [SM.75.799]

www.ingramcontent.com/pod-product-compliance
Lightning Source LLC
Chambersburg PA
CBHW070918270326
41927CB00011B/2625